Unveiling the Secrets

of the

Feminine Principle

Unveiling the Secrets of the Feminine Principle

by

Etta D. Jackson

Email: arcanum33@gmail.com

Phone: +1 917 667-8511

Website: http://www.ancientmysterybooks.com

Book editing: Joye Foderingham

Library of Congress Control Number: 2008904215

International Standard Book No. 0-9746101-3-5

First Edition Published in the United States of America by Lapis Communications

Printed in the United States of America

The Emerald Tablet of Hermes

True, without falsehood, certain and most true, that which is above is as that which is below, and that which is below is as that which is above, for the performance of the miracles of the One Thing. And as all things are from the One, by the mediation of the One, so all things have their birth from this One thing by adaptation. The Sun is its father, the Moon its mother, the Wind carries it in its belly, its nurse is the Earth. This is the father of all perfection, or consummation of the whole world. Its power is integrating, if it be turned into earth.

Thou shalt separate the earth from the fire, the subtle from the gross, suavely, and with great ingenuity. It ascends from earth to heaven and descends again to earth, and receives the power of the superiors and of the inferiors. So hast the glory of the whole world; therefore let all obscurity flee before thee. This is the strong force of all forces, overcoming every subtle and penetrating every solid thing. So the world was created. Hence were all wonderful adaptations, of which this is the manner. Therefore am I called Hermes Trismegistus, having the three parts of the philosophy of the whole world. What I have to tell is completed, concerning the Operation of the Sun.

This book is dedicated to the highest imperfect reflection of the Feminine Principle I had the privilege to know, my Mother, Florence Viviana Jackson, who is now deceased. In my relationship with her, I had the opportunity to see on a daily basis the grace, dignity, compassion, humility, and strength of the feminine in physical form.

Table of Contents

Illustrations

Acknowledgements

I am most grateful to the following people, for their continued support on many levels which has allowed me to carry out my purpose of making this book available to humanity:

Jennifer Anderson of Carlong Publishers: A calming and excellent editor and personality. During our brief meeting your professional knowledge of publishing was invaluable to me. I thank you.

Kevin Bradley: A wonderful friend with whom I can communicate, knowing that he understands my work and mission on this planet and is committed to assisting me in the fulfillment of my destiny.

Joye Foderingham: Your editing insights and help were invaluable. Thanks for both your editing work.

Jilaen Hinds: Thanks for your editorial contribution to this book.

Dwight Lyseight: The calm, professional and detailed manner in which you completed the layout of the book cover and adjusted the cover of my first book, made the experience easy and stress free for me. I am truly grateful and I thank you.

Ebuan Rodgers-Gates: A friend and strong supporter of what she understands to be the Divine Plan for humanity and my role in that plan.

Kathryn Riach: Thank you for volunteering your time to doing the initial editing of this book and for that I am most grateful.

Rick St. Clair: All I can say is that you are a divine gift to my work. Thank you so much.

Ron Walters: You have had an intuitive knowledge of your role in my life and endeavors regarding the publication of my books as evidenced by your remarkable and continued support and goodwill. Your inner knowing of your place in this work entrusted to me shows your true connection to the divine source.

Jacqueline Routier-von Felbert: My daughter and my companion in the long journey that began with your birth, thank you for your editorial assistance with this book as well as with my first book *Understanding Your Choice.*

To my sister *Pauline Jackson- Thomas,* whose insight into the power and purpose of this book and its significance, as intuitively communicated to her by our mother, was invaluable. Thank you also for your support in the cover design.

To my sisters and brothers Basil, Erna, Courtney, Frederick George, Janette, Pauline and Fitz, thank you for rounding out the experience with our mother, which has allowed me to see her true measure.

To my father *Baldwin Eulatima Jackson* who taught all his children the structure of politics and the law, civic responsibility, and how to think constructively, we are eternally grateful. Together with my mother *Florence* who was his perfect complement, they left their children a great legacy of awareness and concern for the less fortunate as well as an understanding of our responsibility and obligation to make a difference in their lives. We have the fondest of memories of both of you as the greatest imperfect earthly reflections of the Divine Masculine and Feminine we could ever hope to have. These memories continue to provide us with lots of laughs even today long after you have left this earthly sphere.

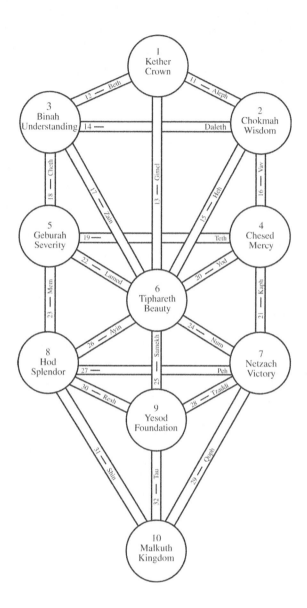

The Tree of Life

The Author's Note

This Age of Aquarius we have just entered marks the beginning of the parting of the veil, which will reveal the true nature of Woman, the Feminine Principle, and the Creative Aspect of the Divine Triad. She took humanity on this long journey eons ago, to experiment and to experience divinity in matter.

Now is the time when men and women are waking up out of their long slumber, and are beginning to remember their purpose and their reason for coming on this adventure into matter. The ancients said that Humanity couldn't be liberated until the memory of the true knowledge and nature of the Feminine was restored, and she assumes her rightful place of power and glory in the external world. Without her there can be no peace, because she is peace itself. She is the link that connects man-to-man, and nation-to-nation. She created everything that is created; she is the Mother of ALL. Nothing in manifestation can exist without her.

The Ageless Wisdom says of her, 'no Man lifts her veil' but only as she finds the individual worthy, will she lift her veil to reveal the long held secret of the relationship of all pairs of opposites— that She and the Father are, in fact, one and the same.

For many people, this information about the Feminine will be unsettling. For too long, Humanity has functioned on half a cylinder, with the Feminine voice muted, and having no meaningful place in the world of men. This is a time of liberation for men as well as women. This adversarial condition between men and women has caused pain and suffering for both gender and has resulted in the delay of true happiness based on equality and the rightful order of things.

The allegories described by St. John in the Christian Bible's Book of Revelation are drawn from every religion of the ancient world. These stories tell us that at the end of the dispensation of the Age of Pisces "The Woman" who is crowned with twelve stars and who was the only one worthy to open "the book" would reveal to Mankind what had been hidden. This she could not do until mankind was able, mentally and emotionally, to comprehend the book. The book is none other than the human body with its three keys and seven locks, a reference to Spirit, which is the three aspects of the Divine triad, and the seven chakras they operate through in the physical form. Only he who has a pure heart and clean hands is in any way ready to hear and to see what she desires to make plain.

Before Jesus left or disappeared, as another school of thought holds, he told his disciples that after his departure the Comforter, the Holy Ghost, would come. I am convinced that this Comforter is the Third Aspect of the Trinity, spoken of in the Zohar, called Shekinah. She, who is the author and creator of all the sacred texts ever written, has held the arcane secrets about humanity's true origin and destiny here on planet Earth. The symbol of the Divine Mother for the Aquarian Age is Isis, the Queen and Goddess of the Egyptian Mysteries. She is the Alchemical Woman, portrayed as nude. She has taken off the robes and veils, which concealed her true identity and her true nature. She now reveals that, all along, she was the Grand Architect and Designer of the Universe. She is the Dark Mother, the Black Pillar in Solomon's Temple whom Mankind calls evil. She formed the light, and created the darkness, and led humanity on a journey into matter. With each step of the involutionary journey Man forgot his relationship to his true place of origin and, his relationship with his brother and sister. The Age of Aquarius, in which Man will walk the Path of Return, characterized as the age of occult mysteries, will bring about a *remembering* of Man's origins, and his true relationship to his fellowman.

In this book, you will begin by recollecting the true relationship of the Mother to the Father, and that one does not, and cannot, exist without the other. In that understanding, you will come to know that the antagonism and feelings of inferiority, and/or superiority between man and woman are at the heart of all internal and external conflicts, and are due to a loss of memory. In chapter two, the Mother is explained as the Geometry of the Universe. She projects out into the manifested world, not only to create a body to *house* the Divine Idea we call Spirit but also to, eventually, merge Spirit and matter in the physical vehicle, the body. The Divine Will was made manifest so that God could dwell with Man and Heaven and Earth would become One; so that the above would manifest as below, and Earth would become a perfect reflection of above.

In Chapter Three, the Divine Mother helps us understand how she spun her web to contain all the elements of the One Life. The Builders of Form on every level of life, work together in

Oneness to establish all the forms through which the Divine Idea's purpose is expressed in the material world.

In chapter four, Water and Liquid Fire are explained. The reader sees the intricate relationship of the Masculine and the Feminine, and understands that separation does not and cannot exist, or there would be no life. The relationship of water to the blood that flows in the body demonstrates the nature of the constitution of Man and explains how the composition and function of the blood aids in the fulfillment of his Divine destiny. The reader can understand that Fire and Water, Male and Female are inseparable, that separation is, in fact, a mental phenomenon and a cleavage of the mind, and that the Mother's focused task in this Age is the healing of the illusion of the belief in separation.

In Chapter five, the Mother reveals the sevenfold or septenate nature of Man: the three aspects of Spirit, and four of matter, and the order that exists on all planes, in all kingdoms, in the Solar System, and the Cosmos. These divisions were established for the purpose of bringing order out of chaos, and establishing Heaven on Earth. Also explained are the seven major ductless glands, which are under the control of the seven major planets of our solar system and the seven complete organs of the heart which by a process of occult anatomy are also present in the brain. The interrelationship of the heart, the brain, the ductless glands together with the solar system, explains how these relationships were established for the purpose of *earthing* spirit in matter.

The mysteries of the heart are revealed in chapter six. Isis, who is described as "The Mother of the Sun," is She who is spoken of in the Book of Revelation as being clothed with the Sun. The three aspects of Spirit externalized are the three-fold nature of the Sun, which is explained as: the Physical Sun, the Spiritual Heart Sun, and the Great Central Sun. When the heart is activated by the Venus force in the body it opens up to a mystical understanding of the true nature of the heart as the center of life. In this awakening of the individual, he comes into full consciousness and the full inflow of the energies of the mid-day sun— the Spiritual Heart Sun.

Chapter seven opens the readers mind up to the Mystery of Shekinah and the Mystery of Sex, which are one and the same. The interplay of the Divine Masculine and the Divine Feminine is the stuff of which we read in the Song of Solomon. Nothing that comes into physicality can manifest outside this sexual dance. All life is continuously in a sexual embrace, and this same sexual energy is responsible for all that is born, and all that dies physically and spiritually. Once this Mystery is understood, the last enemy, "Death", will be conquered.

The final chapter gives the reader an understanding of the three aspects of the Mother: Eve, the mental aspect; Isis, the emotional revealer of the Mysteries of the Heart Initiation; and Mary, the physical aspect, who "earths" the consciousness of the head and the heart into the cells of the body for complete regeneration. The High Priestess explains the journey of Initiation in allegorical form: she is the Female Elder of the Temple, Isis, who reveals to the reader the journey that everyone must take to return to the Father's House. This journey is one taken through the desert on the *feet of understanding,* beginning in the West and leading to the East, the direction, which represents Venus. The journey is esoterically taken on Gimel, the Hebrew name for the Camel that also represents *memory* and is attributed to the High Priestess. The traveler's journey to the Holy Land, Jerusalem, "the Abode of Peace", requires that the traveler *must* sojourn in Egypt.

Every human being yearns for the Holy Land and this provides the urge to journey on, since the desire to visit Jerusalem represents the longing for contentment, the hunger for rest from strife, and the quest for peace. Shekinah alone can take you there, if you but answer her call. She will bestow illumination on all who complete this journey, and Wisdom, not material gold, is the just reward.

Introduction

Over two thousand years ago, the elder brother of the race of man, Yeshua Ben Joseph, the Man we call Jesus, withdrew his presence from outer life. Before he disappeared, he promised that he would return, and this is the time and the season of that return. But who is it that we are we waiting for? Is it the Man Jesus or is it his other aspect, the mate of his being, the High Priestess? Could we be waiting for the one who Jesus said will come to comfort us?

One of Yeshua's final acts before disappearing was to send his disciples into Jerusalem to find a Man carrying a *waterpot*. This, of course, was a glimpse into the Age of the Water Bearer, the Age of Aquarius, of which the waterpot is a symbol. He was indicating here that the element of water would be lifted to a new level. And, esoterically, water is a symbol for the feminine aspect of Being. The source of Water in Qabalistic symbolism represents the Divine Feminine, the Dark Mother, and the Great Ocean, and is also known as the Chief Feminine Elder of the Temple. She is the Pentecost, the Shekinah, and the Holy Ghost. Water holds memory and She is the symbol of water itself. She is also the Book, the container of all memory, which holds the history of the world from the beginning of time. This Book contains the laws that govern all creation.

She, the Book, the Lady Christ and the polar opposite of Yeshua, will disrobe to reveal the secrets She has long held about the true relationships between all pairs of opposites. Her first undertaking is to reveal the truth about the feminine aspect. She will assist humanity in removing the guilt and shame of life, which unfortunately, have been placed at the feet of women. This Dark Mother, the Feminine Principle, is the whore as well as the virgin; she is the daughter and the mother; she is the midwife and the one who gives birth; she is the barren sister; she is the mother of your father and the daughter of your brother; she is the queen upon her throne and the beggar woman on her stool. She is in every woman, and she gave birth to every Man. She is the Feminine Power and Creator behind every created thing.

This woman created what is known as evil, which is no thing other than the act of separating out the dual aspects of the One for the purpose of clarity and understanding. She created apparent darkness, and then immersed herself into it with a third of the host of Heaven in an effort to experience the depth of that reality. That decision was a choice, and the unveiling of this feminine mystery will reveal the reason for that decision to embark on this adventure into matter for the benefit of the planet.

Now, the High Priestess is about to step out of her secret place to reveal the hidden knowledge contained within the Scroll or Book she contains. She has been holding the Scroll unfurled until humanity is mentally and emotionally prepared. The Divine Feminine who brought humanity on this journey of adventure and expansion of consciousness, is the one most qualified to take humanity home. She knows how carefully and meticulously the journey back must be traveled in order to correctly interpret, understand, and integrate every experience.

I invite the reader to approach this book with an open mind and heart and a desire to truly understand the Feminine, since an understanding of the Feminine is integral to an understanding of ourselves. Your soul is the keeper of the mysteries of life. The soul wants to reveal itself to you, and invites you to decipher its profound mysteries in which are hidden the secrets of life. She is your creator, your teacher, your nurturer and sustainer. She is also the destroyer. She tears down what is outworn in your thinking, and then rebuilds you. She molds, refines and transforms you, making you the fit vessel out of which the eternal waters of life will forever flow. Let her have her way with you for she is the builder of your temple. Our Mother will *raise* up all her daughters, of every land and of every race, and restore them to their rightful positions of power. Those who have not slumbered, but have kept their lamps burning, will lead the way toward the redemption of humanity. This is the twelfth hour; it is now mid-night, the hour of the appearance of the Mother.

The Age of Aquarius is the age when women will be restored to their position as it was before the *Fall*, a time of equal power and rulership. Only when equality becomes a reality on our planet, when both men and women feel and understand their own true value, and that of others as well, will the Edenic relationship be restored. Men yearn for this time of oneness, harmony and peace as eagerly as women do, but this cannot be achieved until women awaken to their true position and take their place in the Cosmic Order.

This is an exciting time to be alive, a time when we will see the unveiling of one of the greatest mysteries — that of understanding the truth of the Feminine and the realization of humanity's *only* hope of liberation. For too long, the world has operated at a deficit because the consciousness that created the universe has been held captive in its own creation, which is a result of what happens when there is a loss of memory, allowing for one-half of the whole to be omitted from conscious participation.

Chapter One

WOMAN, WHO ART THOU?

Forget not that these two, the masculine and the feminine
Though they be named superior and inferior
Are in truth of equal rank.
As it is written:
"That which is below is as that which is above,
And that which is above is as that which is below."
Be thou not led astray by their false doctrine
Who ascribe to the inferior nature
Somewhat less of power and worth
Than inherent in the superior.
The two are as the pans of a balance
Each hath its own peculiar quality.
Each hath its appointed sphere of operation.
One cometh not before the other,
But together they exist
From everlasting to everlasting
(Book of Tokens by Dr. Paul Foster Case)

CHAPTER ONE
Woman, Who Art Thou?

The Feminine or Creative Principle is the third aspect of the Divine Trinity. This Trinity consists of the Father, the Son, and the Holy Spirit, who is none other than the Divine Mother. These three aspects comprise what many traditions refer to as God. The sphere of the Great Mother functions, in part, to bring about the best and the fullest expression in form of all that the One Life knows as its fullest potential. She is the Cosmic Principle and also the field of separative activity. She contains in her being both the divine idea for creation and infinite possibilities of form to house the Divine sparks of consciousness that are to be imbedded in matter through the process of involution. A multiplicity of finite specialized forms, are created through the process of multiplication and subdivision. In this act of sub-division, the One Reality does not lose its unity but becomes a fraction of the whole and exists for the purpose of carrying out the divine idea of the Masculine Principle to expand consciousness in matter. Ultimately Spirit emerges out of that dense matter of form by means of the process of the evolution of consciousness, which begins when the Mother allows the individual to experience his first visible, emotional and mental grasp of consciousness. Everything that is recognizable is so, because it has separated itself out from its complementary half, while its other half remains hidden behind in the invisible, un-manifested state. The Divine Mother created this concept of apparent separation in order to give the cognitive mind the ability to understand the concept of Unity.[1]

There is never a time, however, when the Feminine Principle is in objective expression, that the Masculine Principle is not also in a hidden or concealed expression. The idea of separation does not exist in reality; it is a mental construct of creation. The appearance of separation, which we call many-ness, has caused much confusion, pain, and suffering. The twin concepts of the masculine and feminine are inextricably intertwined forever and cannot be separated, or life in creation would cease to be. The masculine or positive charges are in an ongoing sexual dance with the feminine, copulating continuously to produce more and better bodies for the highest expression of consciousness. In order for black to exist, white has to hold it in place. Similarly, in order for a mountain to exist, there must be a valley.

The Principle of Creation is related to the fruit of evil, which is one of the two fruits, that bears on the *one* tree—the Tree of Knowledge of Good and of Evil. The aspect of the Feminine we symbolically identify with Eve carried out the Divine Plan by creating the mental illusion of the reality of matter. So, since the beginning of time, "the woman" has borne the scourge of being "evil" because she dared to offer to take humanity on an adventure. This experience altered the knowledge and understanding humanity, and life in general, would have. Contrary to the accusatory note given by Adam to God in Genesis— that it is "the woman" who was given to him who led him into temptation and caused him to err — the idea of succumbing to the allure of the five senses was always a collective decision of the Godhead and could not have been otherwise. Thus began Man's tendency to find a "scapegoat", to blame in order to avoid taking personal responsibility. The subsequent pain and suffering of Mankind's five-sense experiences is due, in part, to his loss of memory when he fell out of unity.

What we term "God", is really the totality of All Things, and is the No-Thing or Unity out of which all things emanate, and are manifested.[2] The material world is like a Tree of Death, and the mirror of the Tree of Knowledge of Good and of Evil, which is nothing other than, the Tree of Life, which bears these two fruits. All things in creation contain this Tree within it. Conversely, a branch of God or the All's Great Tree of Life is contained within all things. The entire material plane is the result of separation, and is the only visible half of the true Self. The goal of Mankind, therefore, is to restore unity. Man, the greatest act of creation, is the only entity capable of doing this, and this unity can only be achieved in a state of consciousness. Man makes this achievement by withdrawing his consciousness from his attachment to his body with which he has become so identified, and His partaking of the fruits of The Tree of Good and of Evil are evidence of this. He must expand his consciousness until he renders the unconscious part of himself completely conscious. Through this process, he will consciously experience the un-manifested, invisible half of himself, and in so doing, he will then achieve divine unity in his consciousness.[3] Man is, therefore, able to achieve all this while in his body, and He is able merge with the true Self while still in this visible, created world. The achievement of being re-united with his God-self while on the earthly plane is the Mother's reason for taking humanity on this journey. In achieving this, the longing ends and Oneness is realized in the being; thus the all-inclusive cosmic consciousness of unity with all life is then felt and known in the body. This is, in fact, the reason for which humanity exists, even though man is unaware of it.

Everything in creation desires to find its complementary half and to be re-united in wholeness. Even at Man's atomic level, the positive and the negative, male and female, good and evil will seek their other half; but no one will ever find his other half outside of himself in the manifest world[4]

The Divine Feminine is the sphere of Understanding and of Active Intelligence. She is the architect of structure, limitation and order which is manifested as a septenate structure— first as the threefold soul structure and, subsequently, as the fourfold personality vehicle symbolized as a square. This Feminine Principle, the First Cause and undifferentiated cause of all life, set into motion the first cycle which, through its rotation downwards, brought the Divine spark to our planet. As this spark gradually fell into generation, the coat of flesh that encased it became denser with every action.[5]

In the King James Version of the Book of Isaiah 45:6, 7 we are told that light is formed and darkness is created. Creation is a step-down process through which Divine Intelligence in the form of Light descends into matter. The first Light or Primal Fire, the All, is the infused Primordial Intelligent Life that exists throughout creation. The second emanation, the Illuminating Intelligence, is condensed cometary matter and produced forms within the cosmic circle, as it infused the life principle into every form. The third emanation produced the entire universe of physical matter and it created a sevenfold structure in order for the

30

descent of this consciousness to be finally encased in dense matter, or stone. As this spark of intelligent light gradually recedes from the first central divine light, its brightness wanes and it becomes Darkness.[6]

The Divine intent has always been that over the course of time, through the combined efforts of living fire and living water and their reflected glory upon the "water", which is nothing other than liquid stone—the Divine Light encased within — would be drawn out of its prison toward sunlight as a single-celled life-form. This Intelligence, with each turn of the spiral and within each cycle, forever moves upward, reflecting what has always been the ordered and willed intent of the First Cause for the involution and evolution of consciousness. At the end of this journey, the separation between the Life Principle and Matter takes place. As the liberated Spirit gains more and more radiance, it mounts the shining path, which ultimately ends at the point from which it started around the time of the Grand Cycle. Let us now examine the third emanation and her ordered and actively intelligent creation in carrying out the Will and Plan of the First Cause.[7]

Woman is the highest expression of the Cosmic Creative Principle. She is the creator of all life, and all things created are contained in her body. This is the Alchemical Woman called Isis by the Egyptians. She is the recorder of the law, and the form-giving principle. She is also the tamer of the turbulent forces of the animal kingdom. She is the preserver of balance; she is the unveiler of truth, and she is the unveiled truth itself. This Cosmic Mother is the Eternal Dancer, partly hidden by the cyclic forms of cosmic expression. Human consciousness reflects her vision of the higher levels of reality. Because she has been held imprisoned and under a curse for too long, she must now die and be reborn before her powers will find complete expression. Having been subject to Man, and his incorrect knowledge she has been brought lower than the animal and because of that same lying semblance of knowledge, has been crowned with a false authority not her own. This must and will be destroyed before her real powers and real worth may be made manifest, and through herself and her activities, the release shall come.

The Alchemical Mother is the One Worker. For long eons she has been endlessly laboring, spinning, weaving, and making the garments of form in which the One Life clothes itself. In her loom, the tapestry of manifestation has been woven. She is the keeper of the patterns of all possible forms— the cross, the triangle, the square, the pentagon, the hexagon, and the octagon. These are the simple elements for the patterns of all possible forms and together with the circle, which is the container holding all geometric patterns for all the manifold forms in the physical world, they determine all force relations in the universe through the proportions contained in these simple figures.

The work of the Cosmic Mother begins with stars forming themselves into solar systems. We are witness to her achievements by the interplay of activities, which are measurable by the lines and angles that these figures display. Gravity, the most mysterious force of all, operates by a law patterned on these forms, and sound vibration, both in pitch and volume, is determined by the same principles. All the play of light and color follow the same laws of form. Atom mates with atom to build a universe and wherever anything comes into physical manifestation, these same properties are to be found. The Feminine Principle is the matrix of all possible specialized forms of manifestation, establishing limits of quantity, quality, mass, and form. Each form carries within it the note it is to express, and at the same time echoes the unity of all things. Consistent with the intent of Divine Intelligence, the many and varied expressions of the One Life would, at some point in the distant future, come to understand that each is part of something much bigger than itself, but yet identical to itself.

Chapter Two

THE MOTHER -
THE GRAND ARCHITECT
AND DESIGNER

I am the Lord, and there is none else. There is no God beside me.
I girded thee though thou hast not known me.
That they may know from the rising of the sun, and from the West,
that there is none beside me. I am the Lord and there is none else.
I form the Light and create Darkness. I make Peace and create Evil.
I the Lord do all these things. Isaiah 45: 5, 6, 7(KJV)

Shall a trumpet be blown in the city and the people not be afraid? Shall
there be Evil in the city and the Lord hath not done it?
Amos: 3: 6(KJV)

Chapter Two
The Mother ~ the Grand Architect and Designer

The point at which consciousness fell out of unity into matter is what is referred to as *the Fall* of Man. Man can only be reunited with his other half through the spiritualization of matter. Matter must be transformed into Spirit in order for Man to again become whole, and Man is the only entity capable of accomplishing this. He alone of all creatures has developed the physical, emotional, and mental capacity to think, feel, and house this understanding. The Divine spark encased in the tomb of all matter, from the simplest to the most complex life form, is a result of the coming down into matter, and clothing itself with matter and material characteristics. Spirit then animated matter as the Self in order to make possible its spiritualization and salvation. It is through the intellect, the most dangerous and at the same time the greatest gift given to man by Hermes, that man is able to orchestrate his return to divinity. To accomplish this he must build a bridge across the abyss into full conscious union with the "Self", and by means of his intellect, comprehend truth.

The *Emerald Tablet of Hermes* states that in the process of involution, this Divine spark encased itself in stone as it turned into Earth. Qabalistic thought suggests that The Great Mother is associated with the sphere of Saturn, and that since the beginning of time, she has been under the control of Saturn. They also suggest that the solar system was organized by forces operating inward from the great ring of Saturn's sphere. However, the most reasonable inference is that the first forms of worship were dedicated to Saturn whose symbol is the stone. The intrinsic nature of Saturn is synonymous with that of a spiritual rock, the enduring foundation of the solar temple. It has its antitype or lowered octave in the terrestrial rock—planet Earth, which sustains upon its jagged surface the diversified genera of mundane life.[1]

The most familiar Qabalistic representation of the stone is the cube, and the very foundation of form is established on the spiritual principles of the stone cube. In establishing the manifest universe, Saturn, who the Hebrews associate with Binah, the Great Mother, is known as the grand architect who created all forms to make the Divine idea visible on the plane of matter. As the externalization of this idea for a physical universe projected outward into space, there was a very definite and measured way in which this process took shape. The masculine principle at the center of the un-manifested orb remains in balance and perfect harmony as the essence of manifestation projects outward. It is the desire to dwell in the world of form that initiated the need to construct a house, or a clothing of flesh, for this Divine idea. An important aspect in the construction of this form is that it would retain within the vehicle the Divine essence needed to ensure that full recollection would be possible after a long period of forgetfulness in the density of matter, whether we are talking about the great central suns, or the tiniest life form. Every form represents the visible image of the spirit encased inside of it. From the very beginning, when matter separated out or projected out from its source—Spirit, the innate knowledge that both matter in Spirit, and Spirit in matter, would consciously come back together, since Unity was contained in the nucleus of every atom. In fact, all things in manifestation are aspects of the One Reality, and there is no-thing that exists outside of this reality. It therefore follows that what seems to be the multiplication of forms is really the subdivision of the One into various parts, with each part housing a spark of the One Life and destined to express the uniqueness of that spark. The highest expression of matter is Man. He is, in fact, both the creator and the created. Only when Man is able to recognize the creator in himself, will he be able to re-unite with his other half. This is the only way the individual can experience self-knowledge. He must be able to mentally grasp the fact that he and the god who created him are one and the same. He must come to realize that the act of separation is a *mental* one, and once this mental healing takes place, death to separation ceases, and the individual is resurrected as a new Man. Through this experience, he recognizes that the one and only self is the creator of the entire universe.[2]

This process of the realization of Spirit in matter occurs along very definite lines, with numbers and geometric forms expressing this process. Masonry declares "Geometry" to be synonymous with God; since length, breadth, height and depth are the sum total of Life and are God's measure of the dimensions in the three-dimensional world.

Elisabeth Haich, in her book *Initiation,* gives an explanation of how the un-manifest became manifest; of how thought, in essence, became flesh. And the sacred writings of most philosophers and mathematicians, notably, Pythagoras, support her theory. Haich explains that, in order for a force to emerge from the dimensionless state and manifest itself, it needs a point of departure. Manifestation begins with the point (.), which is considered to be the undifferentiated center from which form is initiated on a one-dimensional plane. A point consists of only a single factor and contains within itself the number of unity, the number *one.*

This force whose first manifestation is a point emerges from the dimensionless and moves outward to form a line, giving birth to *length.* Though the line is essentially endless, in the world of manifestation there is always a beginning and an end— a line always involves three factors: its starting point, its end, and the space between the points. The line, therefore, represents the number three, a key number of the one-dimensional world.[3] Clearly, there is no possibility of manifesting or finding the number *two* in unity. When a point moves even the slightest amount, the number *three* is created. The number *two* can only exist when two units are set side by side, and then the number two arises by a kind of splitting of unity. Because nothing has any real existence outside of unity, to manifest itself, it must project a reflection outside of itself. This alludes to the fact that the number *two,* which is usually used to imply *doubt* and creates a kind of fission or separation in the mind and soul, does not really exist and cannot exist outside the three-in -one, or the one-in-three, we call God.

As each of the points of the lines projects outward from itself, the two- dimensional world emerges and gives birth to width.

Out of the totality of these lines, a plane is created giving rise to an equilateral rectangular square, which consists of four lines of force. The rectangle contains five factors, the four manifested lines and the non-manifested area enclosed by the four lines. The key number, then, of the two-dimensional reality is five.

Equilateral rectangle

The three-dimensional world gives rise to height. As the lines of force move outward from the points of the rectangular plane, these lines form a cube. The cube is six-in-one and one-in-six; the six manifested limited planes and the seventh un-manifested factor comprising the whole of the cube. The basic form of matter is cubical, as exemplified by the salt crystal. We now have the emergence of volume.[4]

Always hidden within matter is Spirit, which gave birth to matter in the first place. When a cube is cut obliquely starting from one corner and cutting through to the point on the opposite corner, thus cutting off the corner of the cube, what is exposed is the tetrahedron. In fact, this creates two interlocking tetrahedrons, forming the perfect three-dimensional symbol for God, with four equilateral triangular faces. These four triangular faces are what the sages describe as the four faces of God. The equilateral triangle is the three-dimensional equivalent of the tetrahedron, and representing perfect harmony and perfect equilibrium, as all three points are an equal distance from each other. This is the state of God resting in himself/herself, and therefore corresponds to the three- in- one. However, when force moves out of the dimensionless state of time and space and into the three dimensions, it becomes the creative aspect and manifests itself as four, or three *and* one. The equilateral triangle is viewed as the primordial form of divinity, expressing the three aspects of God. The reader can see that four equilateral triangles are contained within this equilateral triangle.[5] (see diagram)

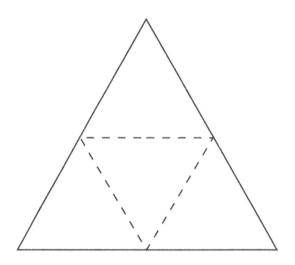

Four- in- one triangle

Robert Lawlor in his book *Sacred Geometry* states that Unity, or the Oneness, contains "the finite Many" because unity exceeds all limitations or descriptions by multiplicity, and at the same time, all limitations by finite conceptual oneness. Unity can be represented as a circle, but the lack of a common measure for the circle, indicates that the circle belongs to a level of symbols beyond reason and measure. The square, which also represents wholeness, lends itself to a better understanding of Spirit. The square represents the four primary orientations of north, south, east and west, and is formed by crossing two pairs of perfectly equal yet oppositional linear elements, thus fulfilling the description of universal Nature described by ancient philosophers.[6]

Physicist Albert Einstein, in differentiating absolute space from relative space indicates that relative space is curved and finite, and states that the arresting of infinite boundless energy, which becomes bound by lines and angles, is what attempts to give physical identity to the entity we call God. As Man evolves through these forms, he is able to return to full conscious identification with Quintessence, his Creator.

Now that we have established the basic geometric forms— the circle, the triangle, and the square, we can see how these three basic forms are configured and bifurcated to produce the five polyhedras, or Platonic solids. These five volumes are essential because all their edges and interior angles are equal. The tetrahedron, the octahedron, the cube, the icosahedron, and the dodecahedron— are only volumetric equivalents of the triangle, the square, and the pentagram, and are solids, which demonstrate how the Many emerged out of the One, by first becoming three, then four, and then five: 1, 3, 4, and 5— the geometric dimensions of the Pythagorean right triangle.[7]

Robert Lawlor explains the Vesica Piscis as a form generator, which has at its center the Pythagorean triangle out of which all regular polygons arise from the succession of vesica constructions. In reality, everything in the created universe is a volume, and the formation of any volume structurally requires triangulation; as such, the trinity is therefore the creative basis of all forms. The Vesica Piscis thus illustrates the geometry of how the Pythagorean triangle makes evident the process of creation and how the "One" became the "Many."[8]

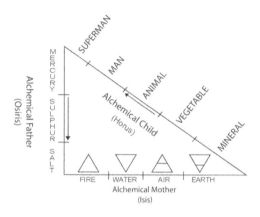

Pythagorean triangle

The Pythagorean triangle also better demonstrates the relationship of the Alchemical Father, the Alchemical Mother, and the Alchemical Child. In his book, *The True and Invisible Rosicrucian Order,* Dr. Case suggests that the Child is asleep in the mineral kingdom; he begins to dream in the plant world and in the animal kingdom, he sleeps on, though sometimes half awake. In Man, the Child awakes and begins to realize the meaning of life. Yet, he has an even higher destiny to fulfill because he is not merely Man—he is God-Man, destined to attain perfect union with the Father. In that union, the alchemical work, or Great Work, is completed. Man finally rises from the limitations of three-dimensional existence to share with his Father and Mother the freedom of the fourth dimension and the immortality of Perpetual Intelligence.[9] This Child is none other than Man, and this potential lies dormant within him.

Keith Critchlow in his book, *Order in Space,* gives a brilliant explanation of the process of how the infinite becomes finite, as well as how Spirit creates appropriate vehicles for operating in matter.

Akasha or Quintessence, represented by the Vesica Piscis, is formed by the intersection of the segments of two circles of equal radius. The Vesica Piscis is produced when the Divine Feminine and the Divine Masculine merge in creation of the "Son or Child," thereby giving expression to their Divine intent to dwell in form. The Pythagorean triangle expresses how this Divine Idea (Word) for living in flesh became a reality in each of the four kingdoms. First, it manifests as the element of fire, and then continually wraps itself in a clothing of flesh, making it possible for spirit to dwell in the dense vibration of matter. These manifestations may be two-dimensional, three-dimensional, and even four-dimensional[10] The same units, which make up the three sides of the Pythagorean triangle, eloquently illustrate the union of the Alchemical Father—the principles of Sulphur, Mercury and Salt, in union with the Alchemical Mother—the elements of: Fire, Water, Air and Earth. These elements then give birth to the Alchemical Child, the Sun/Son, the kingdoms of—the mineral, vegetable, animal, human and, finally, God-Man, the Regenerated Man. The five Platonic solids are the houses of the five elementals of: ether, fire, water, air, and earth, in the five kingdoms.

Rama Prasad's book *Nature's Finer Forces,* explains that these elements proceeded out of pure Spirit, which he also calls Quintessence or Akasha and that these five elements also refer to the five realities or principles that express the actual intelligences of the One Life.

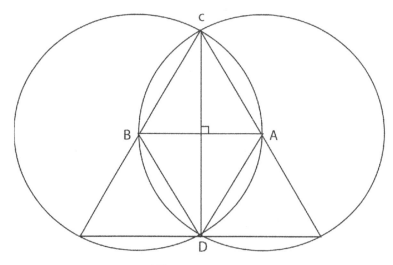

The Vesica Piscis

These elements: Ether, Fire, Water, Air and Earth are subdivisions of Spirit, and each is associated with a sense and color.

- Ether/Ether with the sense of hearing or sound vibration, and the color black/blue-violet
- Ether/Fire with the sense of sight and the color red
- Ether/Water with the sense of taste, and the color white/violet
- Ether/Air with the sense of touch and the color blue/greenish
- Ether/Earth with the sense of smell and the color yellow, which is a synthesis of sensations.

While sensations are not the same as reality itself, they do give Man the notion of substance and therefore his experience of the third dimension.

The following five basic forms are also related to each of the five elements. They are —the Tetrahedron, the Octahedron, the Cube, the Icosahedron, and the Dodecahedron.

The relationships are as follows:

- Fire —Tetrahedron
- Air —Octahedron
- Earth —Cube
- Water —Icosahedron
- Ether —Dodecahedron

In Eastern philosophy, these five forms or principles, called Tattwas are classified as: Teja, Vayu, Prithivi, Apas, and Akasha, respectively.(see chart)   Every form is designed and constituted in such a way as to give maximum expression to the spirit of consciousness that is encased in it. The objective is to be able to experience God in matter and to mentally and emotionally make meaning of the experiences of life in that form, so as to have total knowledge of the embodiment of God in matter. This experience gives birth to the dwelling of God in the kingdom of *flesh*.[11] An important understanding of this journey of humanity's unfoldment is that Man's complete self-knowledge can only be achieved through his mental and emotional understanding of his life experiences. The ability to *know* through *feeling* is essential, and without this component, his achievement is incomplete because we gain our awareness of Spirit, or Quintessence, from experiencing the operation from which the other four elements fire, water, air and earth arise. Since nothing exists outside of Spirit, whether life is expressing itself in form or formlessness, it exists continuously in pure spirit. We are afforded the opportunity through our senses, of a relative experience with Spirit, and through the steady process of Initiation, Man comes to know Spirit through the union that occurs. In alchemy, this process and accomplishment is called, the Great Work.

Everything in existence, and in one's universe, is a fraction of the unknown One. Though the concept of ONENESS seems unthinkable, Man's contemplation of this philosophical concept, coupled with his mystical experiences, forces him, a traditional thinker, to place this idea at the forefront of his thought process. As he becomes more reflective, he is able to relate all parts to one another proportionally in order to achieve *knowing*. It is multiplicity that, in fact, reveals Unity, and Unity creates by dividing itself. The circle, being the symbol of Unity, is the container of all that exists and, at the same time, all that has not yet manifested in form—and on the plane of matter, the circle manifests as the supernal triangle. When lowered or projected out, it appears as the square— demonstrating the four elements of fire, water, air and earth, which are the composites of matter. It is this concept of the triangle and the square that gave rise to Man as a septenate being. He is Spirit represented by the triangle sitting on the square— the tetrahedron, which gave birth to the cube.[12] The Golden Section, or the Extreme and Mean Proportion, expresses the sovereign and creative nature of Man who was given dominion over the Earth in the Garden of Eden. It also demonstrates the relationship of — *the Lesser to the Greater, and the Greater to the Whole.*

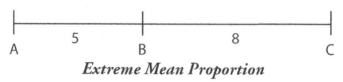

Extreme Mean Proportion

Mathematicians and philosophers assign the values of 5 units to the smaller segment, 8 units to the larger and 13 units to the whole line, which yields the golden ratio of ~1.6 by dividing the larger by the smaller. This is the *constant* for all life in the manifested universe. The life-force created by this ratio is continual in creation and is the basis for the movement of logarithmic spirals. These spirals are the basis for all forms, from the single-cell organism to the lion in the jungle, to Man, the crowning achievement of creation. It is only by relating all parts to one another proportionately that knowing is achieved and these proportional relationships are aimed at leading the mind back to Oneness. The extremes of AB and AC are bound together by BC. The Greeks call this a continuous proportion of three terms where one element is to a second as the second is to the third; this, in turn, gave rise to the term "analogy." In this proportionality, the relationship of nature (AB) to Man (BC) corresponds to the relationship of Man (BC) to God (AC) which is AB + BC. In this relationship, Man is the central figure and thus becomes both the perceiver and the identity between the observed differences and the extreme.

Man, does not stand outside the comparative activity, but is himself the orchestrator. Man is able to register in his cells, the experiences of his environment as vibrational patterns from his field of awareness. He is able to interpret and distinguish between the external vibratory field and the inner field of perceptions. This is the evolution of consciousness or the mode of perpetual awareness that Sri Aurobindo describes as knowledge by identity, and this development is an important stage in the process of spiritual development.[13]

The geometric proportion of these two terms, 5 and 8, which yields the number 1.6183 has also been given the name *Golden*

Proportion, and is designated by the Greek letter phi (φ). This irrational number 1.6183 expresses the geometric progression, relating the internal original ideation to the reflected external plane of manifestation. Lawlor cites the *Upanishads* as saying that, "It is through the perceiver, Man, a symbol of the Son of God, that all things take on their existence from that which perceives them."

When the mathematical concept of the Golden Proportion is fully understood, the evidence for how the Trinity — 'Three, that is Two; and Two that is One' — gives proof of the causal singularity through the ultimate reduction of proportional thought, will be fully grasped. The concept of the relationship of "many-ness" to the One will then finally become evident since it is the irrationality of the number of the Golden Proportion that provides for the perpetuation of creation.[14]

The encasement in which "spirit" or the "spark of life" is entombed in the stone sepulchre of form is called a vault. This vault or tomb is said to have seven sides, each with dimensions of five feet by eight feet. Mathematical and scientific evidence suggests that these rectangular sides of 5 by 8 produce what is called the Golden Mean Rectangle. The Golden Mean Rectangle later becomes the *sarcophagus* that liberates the spirit from the prison of matter at the final Initiation.[15]

Through his theorems, Pythagoras illustrated how the Feminine Principle uses the laws of geometry to elucidate the science by which her powers are measured. The proportion of 5:8 is the nearest arithmetic expression of the Pythagorean Golden Section, or Extreme and Mean Ratio, which is defined as that division of a quantity which makes the ratio of its lesser part to its greater part, the same as the greater part is to the whole. This is the same proportional relationship of Nature to Man, and Man to

God.[16] The logarithmic spiral illustrated below represents the basis of all forms. At the basis of the logarithmic spiral is the Golden Mean Rectangle. As the spiral expands, the dimensions of the original structure remain constant. The nebulae from which our solar system evolved are formed through the interplay of activities measurable by the lines and angles displayed by these many figures and their proportions. The Golden Mean Proportion is derived from this spiral, and all things in creation come into manifestation through the strict cosmic geometric principle of triangulation. The Alchemical Woman works with the same patterns by means of what is called gnomonic expansion. She uses these geometric operations as the basis for the formation of spiral curvatures, which serve as the model for a vast range of universal movements, from particles to galaxies.[17]

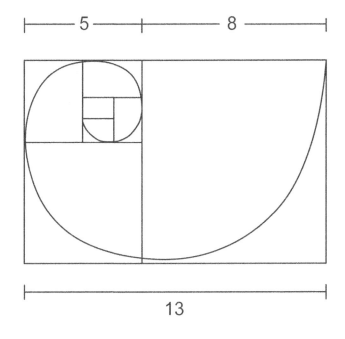

Logarithmic Spiral

It is through the application of the alchemical process to the geometry of human form that these patterns become the key to accomplishing the Great Work in Man. When the human mind is turned inward toward recognition of the structure of the body, with the aid and influence of Spirit upon sub-consciousness— the builder of forms— Man will also become conscious of the actual re-construction of his subtle and gross physical vehicles. He will then understand how the Child is born in him, the same Child whose destiny is union with his Father; the Child who is Master of all things in heaven and earth.[18]

The Grand Architect designed the human form meticulously and precisely according to Divine specifications, in such a way as to allow the Designer to fall asleep in it. And with continuous, vibratory impulses from his soul, Mankind will eventually awaken to full consciousness and become a witness to his inheritance of the Kingdom of Heaven.

The Five Platonic Solids - Tattwas of the East

Tetrahedron			Color	Sense	Element
			Red	Sight	Fire-Teja
Octahedron					
			Blue/ Greenish	Touch	Air-Vayu
Cube					
			Yellow	Smell	Earth-Prithivi
Icosahedron					
			White/ Violet	Taste	Water-Apas
Dodecahedron					
			Blue/ Violet/ Black	Hearing/ Sound Vibration	Ether-Akasha/ Quintessence

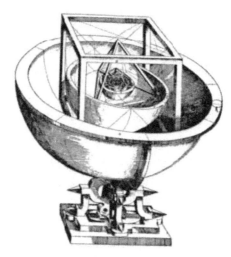

Kepler's vision

Johannes Kepler who was a German Lutheran mathematician, astronomer and astrologer, was a key figure in the astronomical revolution of the seventeenth century; and is best known for his three kinematical laws of planetary motion. Kepler claimed to have had an epiphany on July 19, 1595 while teaching a class in Graz, where he was demonstrating the periodic conjunction of Saturn and Jupiter in the zodiac. He found that each of the five Platonic solids could be uniquely inscribed and circumscribed by spherical orbs nesting these solids, each encased in a sphere within one another would produce six layers, corresponding to the six planets known at the time: Mercury, Venus, Earth, Mars, Jupiter, and Saturn. Kepler found that by ordering the solids correctly—the octahedron, icosahedron, dodecahedron, tetrahedron, and the cube, the spheres could be placed at intervals corresponding to the relative size of each planet's path, assuming the planets circle the Sun.

Kepler's first law— the Law of Eclipses, states that all planets orbit the sun in a path, which resembles an eclipse, with the sun being

The Mother - the Grand Architect and Designer

located at one of the foci of that ellipse. His second law, referred to as the Law of Equal Areas describes the speed at which any given planet will move while orbiting the sun; and that the speed at which any planet moves through space is always changing, and moves the fastest when it is closest to the Sun. His third Law of Harmonics compares the orbital period and radius of the orbit of a planet to those of other planets.

Chapter Three

GRANDMOTHER SPIDER'S WEB

"In the beginning, there was the dark purple light at the dawn of being.
Spider Woman spun a line to form the East, West, North, and South.
Breath entered Man at the time of the Yellow Light.
At the time of the Red Light, Man proudly faced his creator.
Spider Woman used the clay of the Earth, Red, Yellow, White,
and Black to create people.
To each she attached a thread of her web,
which came from the doorway at the top of her head.
This thread was the gift of creative wisdom.
Three times she sent a great flood to destroy those
who had forgotten the gift of her thread.
Those who remembered floated to the new world and climbed to safety
through the Sipapu Pole, the womb of Mother Earth."
~ Navajo Creation Story ~

CHAPTER THREE
Grandmother Spider's Web

Common amongst the creation stories of all indigenous groups is the oral tradition of how the feminine creative principle meticulously brought order out of the chaos of exploding stars; this occurrence, in effect, brought into manifestation a place where life and consciousness could incubate and grow.

The phenomenon of the world-wide-web is not a modern concept. As all indigenous cultures of the world who consider themselves keepers of the Earth know, the Earth with its net holds all humanity and all life forms together. The electro-magnetic grid that envelops the planet is created by longitudinal and latitudinal lines forming the web within which the creative principle operates, as it distributes the incoming impulses sent to the planet for the evolution of humanity, and all life forms.

Among indigenous groups, the Planet is regarded as a living entity with its major and minor centers of force, designed to act as conduits for the distribution of these impulses. Our planet together with the other six major planets, form a cosmic unity into which these planets' energies and forces pour in from certain great constellations.

The etheric web, composed of etheric matter specific to the physical plane, is described as a network that is penetrated and animated with fire or golden light. Under the direction of the Builders of Form, the shape of the web is established and built by fine interlacing strands of this etheric matter. This structure then becomes the scaffold upon which the dense physical body is modeled, and under the Law of Attraction the denser matter of the physical plane coheres to this vitalized form. The gradual build up of this physical matter around and within the etheric form continues until the interpenetration is so complete that the two forms become one unit. This network of etheric matter is a counterpart to the nervous system and its ganglia of the human body.[1]

The impact of the pranic emanations of the etheric web around the physical body is comparable to the effect of the sun on the physical planet. And in fact, these bodies are just one system of transmission and interdependence within a vast system. An individual's etheric body is not an isolated and separated human vehicle but is, in a special sense, an integral part of the etheric body of that entity which we call the human family and, through his etheric body, he is also an integral part of the planetary etheric body. In the same way, the etheric body of our planet is not separated from the etheric bodies of other planets, and all of them in their totality, along with the etheric body of the sun, constitute the etheric body of the solar system. The field of space itself is etheric in nature and its vital body is composed of the totality of the etheric bodies of all constellations, all solar systems, and all planets found within it.[2]

The etheric web is composed of the cosmic, planetary, and human web of light and is essentially a web of triangles. In the beginning, a pattern of squares provided the major construction but as the work of the Divine Plan unfolded, these squares were bisected and transformed into triangles. The etheric web that results is an intricate, constantly moving, interwoven series of triangles. From each point of any triangle there emanates three lines or streams of energy, a total of nine streams for each triangle. This process leads to the spiritualization of all forms and the evolution of consciousness.[3] Due to the constant, onward, interior, and revolving movement everywhere in the solar system and the zodiac, the coordinated and organized movement of the web's power to qualify and condition the entire universal pattern is possible.

There are seven cosmic, planetary, and human centers or vortices of energy, with their resulting forty-nine sub-levels in each body, and through the interrelationship of their triangular designs, one can appreciate the great beauty of this magnificent dance. The etheric web provides the vehicle through which physical forms are related to the physical planet and to the human vehicle. The divine intelligences that work in the four kingdoms are the builders of this form. The four elementals are:

- The salamanders, who work with the element fire
- The undines, who work with the element of water
- The sylphs, who work with the element of air
- The gnomes, who work with the element of earth

The Grand Architect designs and supervises the command, which includes the note and the tone of each form to be manifested, and through which the mineral, vegetable, animal, and human kingdoms all came into being. In the building of the human form, its construction is impacted by the racial and group karma to be played out in each incarnation. Moreover, the group within which an individual will operate determines the involvement by builders from elemental builders, which fall into two groups and are of various colors and kinds. Violet is the predominant color and the signature color of the Age of Aquarius in which we now live. It is significant to note that the Age of Aquarius is the age of synthesis in which we will see a merging of the masculine (red) and the feminine (blue), a reality of union in consciousness.

The intricate process that creates the etheric web, and gives rise to the physical world is a fascinating one. Form is produced in response to:

- *Divine thought* from the cosmic mental plane, which conditions the head center in the body
- *Divine desire* from the cosmic astral plane, which conditions the throat center
- *Divine activity* from the cosmic physical plane, which consists of our seven systemic planes and conditions the heart center.[4]

Everything in creation possesses a mental, astral/emotional, and physical body and these three bodies together constitute the personality or, more appropriately, the personality vehicle of the entity. The two groups critical to the process of creation are described in occult phraseology as *the listening builders* and the *seeing elementals*.

The *listening intelligences* pick up the note and tone from those who transmit the sound to the physical plane and this sound allows the *builders* to gather the substance for the intended material form. They are referred to as having *ears* but are not able to *see* and so they work in close cooperation with the dense physical body.

The second group, the *seeing elementals*, exists on the three lower sub-planes in matter and, in an occult sense they are able to *see* on the objective plane. This type of *seeing* is an analogy between sight and knowledge.[5]

The Builders of Form fall into six primary categories:

1. The Builders of Human Vehicles
2. Those who build the forms in the three kingdoms below man—the mineral, the vegetable and the animal kingdoms.
3. The Builders of the Planetary Etheric Web—their work is extremely obscure and concerned with the materialization, preservation and destruction of the planetary web
4. The Builders of the Etheric Body of the Planetary Entity
5. The Builders of the Planetary Body
6. The Etheric Doubles of all that Man creates

As consciousness evolves, a more expanded and appropriate vehicle for the embodiment of that new reality is created.

The intricate process of building bodies for the manifestation of the Divine on the plane of matter merits extensive study. Conscious Man, who is described as a crystallized ray of the One Life, has worked through the process of evolution into what is known as human being. He then becomes co-creator on the plane of matter by directing the appropriate building of forms in the kingdoms in nature. Man, a sevenfold entity is so constituted that in the three permanent centers of force are hidden the three primary fires of substance, which contain all spiritual potentialities. These three forces of energy are held in the causal sheaths and give rise to the fourfold physical body.[6] At his final initiation, Man is liberated from the bondage of ignorance and becomes a sevenfold conscious being.

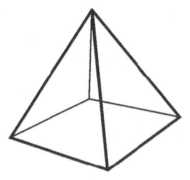

The Pyramid, a symbol of septenary Man

The process of physical plane creation includes the embodiment of a thought or an idea. The sound of the *note* and the *tone*, influenced by the power of thought, determines the sheath to be built around this idea. We can then see the quality, psychic nature, aroma, emanation or magnetism of *the Thinker* working itself out through the form since all form, though temporary, comes into existence under the direction of *the Thinker* and as a function of necessity. When that function is fulfilled, and all possibilities are exhausted, the *Thinker* withdraws its attention from the form. As previously stated, every form becomes manifest in response to an "idea" that needs to come onto the physical plane. This process occurs when the *sound* from the sphere of the Mother, issued to the *Son of Necessity*, reverberates on the physical plane and produces physical incarnation. In relation to the physical plane, the human being is an Etheric Being—he is the one who manifests the kingdoms below him and the Builders who embody the Plan and direction of the Soul/*the Thinker* respond by constructing the fabric of the body. The Builders first construct the sheaths through which the soul is to express itself; then, they build the real form out of etheric substances to produce the sheath of intricate lines of interlaced fiery strands, which are extensions of the life-thread. The work of the Builders reaches consummation when the Life Thread of the Soul is connected to the three centers in the head—the pineal, the pituitary, and the throat center. The seventh center, the pineal, is the most important of these, being the center from which the life of the etheric body withdraws at the time of death. There is no permanence in the causal sheath, so the seventh principle of each sheath gathers to itself the achieved qualities and stores them up, since under the Law of Action and Reaction, it will resurface again and be demonstrated as the plane impulse at each fresh cycle of manifestation.

As forces are withdrawn from the lower centers of the human entity and the globe, the Regenerated Man will cease to be interested in physical incarnation and will function on a greater cosmic level. When Man appreciates his position as Creator, the process of sexual reproduction on the physical will give way to creation on the mental plane and the sex organs will be viewed differently, as creation will eventually become the result of thought impulses, not desire impulses. Creation on the physical plane will be in response to the idea of concrete and energetic embodiments, which will become a reality when Man is able to fully grasp the functions of the etheric body, as it is scientifically understood, from an occult perspective.[7]

The process of the evolution of consciousness is at the basis of the construction of the human vehicle. Man's physical body is designed to receive the fires of spiritual consciousness coming from the three egoic or soul forces into his etheric body. He will only be able to function consciously in his etheric body when each unit of consciousness through self-induced effort burns through that web. At that point, he is able to achieve the goal and cross the *burning ground* into a microscopic portion of his etheric web. Once all the units or cells in his body have achieved full knowing—he is set free from the density of matter and ignorance on all levels of consciousness.[8]

The human entity and Earth are intertwined in a relationship geared toward the achievement of illumination. The human entity is considered by the Masters of Wisdom to be unenlightened and on a path destined to leave his state of unconsciousness to become a fully conscious, self-knowing being. Likewise, Earth, which is also a living entity, is destined to leave its non-sacred state to become sacred, and to become a star. A planet becomes sacred when the center at the symbolic base of the spine of the planet is aroused and a great fusion of energies results. This center is none other than the Saturn center, one of the seven centers in the body. Fusion must be with a sacred planet, and the planet must aid the process of affecting fusion between soul and body—between consciousness and form— thereby producing the quickening of intuition.

The relationship of the planet Venus to the planet Earth is analogous to the relationship of Man's soul or Higher Self, to his personality for it is through the medium of the etheric web that Venus carries out her work of spiritualizing the physical planet. It is not possible to speak to the evolution of consciousness of planet Earth or the human entity without serious consideration of the planet Venus. The three basic functions of the etheric web are to receive, assimilate, and transmit prana, or the life-breath, and the three qualities of the soul, which must be impressed upon the etheric web for the evolution of consciousness, are:

- Spiritual Will
- Spiritual Love
- Knowledge

What emerges then, is not only the knowledge that in order for both the Earth and Man to accomplish the goal of becoming "sacred," the soul and the body must merge, and also that the Saturn centers in the bodies of both Man and the Earth are vital to this accomplishment.

An understanding of the relationship between the soul and the personality (which consists of the physical, emotional, and mental bodies) is key to the outcomes of physical, emotional and mental liberation of both, for without this the liberation of the personality cannot be achieved. So, against this backdrop, let us examine the physical and energetic structures of Venus and the Earth, particularly with regard to the Saturn centers, which facilitate the unfoldment of consciousness.

Saturn, Neptune and Uranus are related to permanent atoms in the causal body of Man. A permanent atom is a unit of energy operating within the sphere of the soul. These atoms are like memory cells and they store the past memory of the personal self. Permanent atoms are the repositories of past experiences contained in the nucleus of the cell that reflect the "quality" and the "note" the body is able to achieve. Saturn corresponds to the physical, Neptune to the astral, and Uranus to the mental atom, but the significance of the Saturn center, through its vibrational impact on the processes of both the body and the entity, is critical.

Saturn known as the Lord of Karma or Action and Reaction, is said to have *followed the sons of Man down into their low place*. It's power is completed when humanity has freed itself from the Wheel of Karma, the Whirling Cross of Material Change, and the Fixed Cross of Illumination and Consciousness. On the esoteric level, Saturn is unable to follow Man onto the Cardinal Cross of the Adept because at that point Man has already freed himself from the Wheel of Karma.

Saturn creates opportunities for change in the life of the individual and the planet, by initiating points of crises, and setting the stage for choices to be made. At these points, determination becomes inevitable, and Saturn conditions each point in evolution where choice definitely becomes possible and allows for conscious acceptance or rejection of that choice.[9]

In an occult sense, Venus is said to be the *alter ego* of the Planet Earth and her role is crucial to the transformation of this physical, non-sacred planet. In addition, Venus is responsible for the regeneration and enlightenment of the human being, who is now walking the Path of Return. Venus plays a central role in the four planetary systems of Gemini, Virgo, Sagittarius and Pisces in order to bring about the spiritualization of these bodies. These four mutable signs also represent mutable Air, Water, Fire and Earth, respectively, and function on the four arms of the Whirling or Mutable Cross. The Mutable Cross, which is the Cross of the Holy Spirit or the Third Person of the Christian Trinity, organizes substance and evokes sensitive response from substance itself. The Man who is crucified upon this Cross suffers, agonizes, desires, strives, and is the apparent victim of circumstances—his experience being distinguished by a veiled vision and incipient longings."[10]

Pisces, ruler of the Age we have just left, and whose influences we are still experiencing, creates these physical, emotional and mental bodies in which Man has this regenerative experience. Cellular knowledge is assigned to the sign of Pisces, making this the force within the cells that establishes Corporeal Intelligence and has responsibility for the process of generation in the body. In order for an individual to be regenerated, the energy in the reproductive center in his body must reverse its course; the physical reproductive focus must give way to an emphasis on creative reproduction on the mental plane. Pisces must prepare the human and planetary vehicles to receive into their etheric webs the inflow of the light from Venus. The regenerative process was most potent during the last phase of the Piscean Cycle, under Scorpio's influence, when Pluto's influence was exerted in the last decanate. This is the reason that humanity as a whole, has now set foot on the Path of Return.

Jupiter and Neptune rule Pisces, but as Venus is exalted, it has its strongest influence in this sign. Neptune, one of the newly discovered planets has, in a sense, has become the co-ruler with Jupiter, which was the former singular ruler of Pisces, and focuses the influence of Pisces as it concerns humanity as a whole and not just the individual Man. Mankind is now ready, for the first time and in large numbers, to be positioned for World Discipleship, and his first major initiation. In this same regard, the symbol for the sign of Pisces, the Fishes, bound together and displayed in opposition to each, symbolizes the captivity of the soul in form. But it is the influence of Pluto, in the last decanate of Pisces that symbolically *"cuts the thread which binds the two opposing lives together."*

Venus is the ruler of the constellation of Gemini, the sign of the Twins. Under this sign, the desire of the pairs of opposite is revealed and this, in fact, is the underlying theme of the entire creative and evolutionary process, as well as the interplay of the opposites. Gemini also symbolizes that duality, in which Venus *"reunites the severed lives but with no binding thread."* Because of the changeable and fluid nature of Gemini, the great shifts in consciousness that are produced, distinguish the disciple from the initiate. Pisces rules the feet; the part of the body most associated with understanding, and this is why the path of enlightenment or the Path of Return must be walked, figuratively and literally, on the feet. For it is through walking and the physical contact with Mother Earth that humanity reaches an understanding of life.

This brings to mind the journey of the prodigal son. The glorification of the Path is achieved by bringing about the waning of the power of form and the waxing of the life of the soul due to the one-pointed soul effort of the sign of Sagittarius, which is governed esoterically by Mother Earth.[11]

As the influences of Gemini, Virgo Sagittarius and Pisces are eventually fused and blended, the Cross must become the line, and then the point. Venus links Man-to-Man, Nation-to-Nation, and Spirit to Matter, and it is under the influence of these four forces of Gemini, Sagittarius, Virgo, and Pisces, that Venus conditions the mind. Through the power of the mind, reason is transmuted into wisdom by the instrumentality of Love. Venus is therefore able to bring about responsiveness and recognition in the body, which conditions Man's consciousness, preparing him to transfer off the Mutable Cross, mount the Fixed Cross of chosen crucifixion and, finally, to die to the allure of matter. As difficult and painful as this process may be, it is the most beneficent way, in which the man on the Return Path is able to accomplish illumination.

However, it is Saturn that applies the limitation, the pressure, and the restrictions on the etheric form, making it possible for Venus to bring about the transformative work, which is achieved through the network of light provided by the etheric web and its counterpart, the nervous system and its ganglia. The pressure exerted by Saturn on the etheric envelope causes a rupture in the top of the head, allowing the light from Venus to pour into the body, and bringing about a merging of the body with the Soul. Having provided the opportunity and created the crisis for the aspirant, Saturn moves Man to the Cardinal Cross, the Cross of Resurrection, where he will meet the tests and trials of Initiation. At this point Saturn, the Lord of Karma and of Retribution, has completed its task in the human's life; and has exacted full payment for the karmic debt owed by the aspirant; the aspirant is now finally free, because Saturn cannot follow him onto the Cardinal Cross.

In summary, the etheric web is:

- The mould of the physical body.
- The archetype upon which, under the direction of Venus, the dense physical form is built, whether it relates to the solar system or the human body.
- A network of interlacing channels, formed from the matter of the four ethers, (fire, water, air, and earth) which is the focal point for the radiatory emanations that vitalize, stimulate and produce the rotary action of matter.
- The etheric scaffolding and framework upon which dense matter is built.
- A barrier between the physical and astral planes. This barrier is penetrated to allow the being, which has evolved in consciousness, to escape beyond the limits of the dividing web, freeing the individual from the limits of personality influence.
- The Facilitator of the manifestation of the Divine energy into dense matter. Whether on the cosmic, planetary, or human level, there must be an organ to receive this life-breath. On the cosmic level, the sun is the receiving organ; on the planetary level, Saturn is that organ; and on the

human level, the spleen is that organ. The distribution of this pranic energy over each of these bodies determines the health of the body, which is then visible in the auric field of the individual.

- The vehicle, which allows for the manifestation of the divine idea in form, and who nurtures that idea, bringing it to maturity; it then oversees its death to the attachment of form, and finally its resurrection back into oneness with its Divine Source.

- When Man, the Thinker and the Knower, withdraws his attention from his "little planetary system" and the "will to live" vanishes, the physical body begins a process of disintegration as he withdraws through the top of the head of the radiant etheric body. As the framework disintegrates, the dense physical form falls apart, the pranic life is abstracted from the dense sheath and the stimulation of the fires of matter ceases.

There is a close connection between the spleen, the top of the head, and the etheric body. It is through the spleen, via the umbilical cord, that the infant receives nourishment from its mother until it is severed at birth. At death, when the interlaced cord of the etheric matter is broken, the silver cord is loosened, and Man severs his connection with his dense physical body, and then passes out through the highest center of the body. The same procedure takes place on the planetary level.[12]

The level of consciousness attained by the individual determines the center from which the life force exits the body. When an individual's consciousness is focused above his diaphragm, he is well on his way to enlightenment. There are actually three places in the body where the life force exits: the crown of the head, the heart, and the solar plexus. These three centers are protected during one's lifetime by an additional thin layer of etheric matter. At the time of death, the pulsation of the energy in the body against the web of either of these exit points, or orifices, ruptures and allows for the release of the life force. The evolved person, the initiate and rational thinking being, exits from the fontanel in the region of the brain. At the time of illumination, the individual at a similar level of evolution experiences a rupture that occurs in the same region of the brain, allowing light to come into the brain and establishing a continuous stream of consciousness. The kindly, well-meaning, intelligent, philanthropic good citizen, exits through a small aperture at the apex of the heart. The lesser evolved, emotional, unintelligent, unthinking person, and those in whom the animal nature is strong, exits from the solar plexus.[13] The individual who experiences a rupture of the etheric web in the solar plexus during early childhood drifts in and out of his physical body into the lower astral planes; this is the case with many lower-level psychics.

I am certain that Tim Bernes-Lee who, created the world-wide-web, did so under the impulse, influence and direction of Venus, Uranus and Neptune. Venus the planetary Mother is responsible for connecting Man-to-Man and Nation-to-Nation. Uranus is the ruler of the Aquarian Age, and the master of new and original technology, and it is Neptune, who brings about expression on the physical plane. It is therefore through this collaboration that the web was made manifest.

The Christ Consciousness in Man is now being born in the sign of Capricorn, the sign of Initiation, which brings the stubborn, unyielding, cruel and ruthless aspirant to his knees under the harsh law of Saturn. This Christ consciousness is initiating an era of intelligent brotherhood under the influence of Venus, so that the new Christed humanity becomes the World Server in Aquarius, and the Piscean World Saviors can then declare the work finished, when the work of regeneration is complete.[14] The world-wide-web was created to aid in this objective.

"Father-Mother spin a web whose upper end is fastened to Spirit, the Light of the One Darkness; and the lower end to Matter, Spirit's shadowy end; this web is the Universe spun out of the two substances made in One, which is the one substance.

As a spider throws out and retracts its web, as herbs spring up in the ground, so is the Universe derived from the un-decaying One. The germ of unknown Darkness, is the material form which all evolves and develops, as the web from the spider, as the foam from the water.

The Web expands when the Breath of Fire, the Father, is upon it; it contracts when the Breath of the Mother, the Root of Matter, touches it. Then the Sons, the elements with their respective Intelligences, dissociate and scatter, to return into their Mother's bosom at the end of the Great Day and becoming reborn one with her. When the Web is cooling, it becomes radiant, its sons expand and contract through their own selves and hearts; they embrace infinitude."[15]

Chapter Four

WATER, THE GREAT MOTHER AND FATHER

The Root of Life was in every drop of the Ocean of Immortality,
and the Ocean was Radiant

Light, which was Fire, and Heat, and Motion.
Darkness vanished and was no more; It

disappeared in its own essence, the body of Fire and Water,
or Father and Mother.

Light is Cold Flame, and Flame is Fire,
and Fire produces heat, which yields Water:

The Water of Life in the Great Mother.

The Secret Doctrine, H. P. Blavatsky, Vol. 1, p. 29

CHAPTER FOUR

Water,
The Great Mother
and Father

"True, and without falsehood, certain and most true......
concerning the Operation of the Sun, all things are from the One,
by the mediation of the One, so all things have their birth from
the *One Thing* by adaptation. The Sun is its Father, and the Moon
its Mother. Thou shalt separate the earth from the fire, the subtle
from the gross, suavely and with great ingenuity."[1]

The book of Genesis, a poetic Hebrew synthesis of creation
stories, begins with the separating out of the two aspects of the
One Reality— Heaven and Earth. When the Life-Breath brooded
upon the waters and separated the superior from the inferior,
this act established the first pair of opposites. The mental image
one gets is that of a vast abyss of fluid darkness that is without
form and void. Philosophers and alchemists alike, state that the
intrinsic nature of Earth is real emptiness, and the intrinsic nature

of space is the real earth-essence. Isaiah 45:6, 7(KJV), states that God created the darkness, and formed the light. The superior term was given to Heaven as that which is above, and the inferior term was given to Earth, as that which is below; thus marking the first distinction between Heaven and Earth.

This separation was not the production of something from nothing, but rather the establishment of divisions, distinctions, and boundaries, all the while maintaining the Reality of Unity. The superior term Heaven was designated as masculine and associated, with the sky or space, while the term Earth was designated as feminine, and was associated with the Earth. The term, Heaven, is synonymous with *God* and with *Creative Thought, the Word,* and the superior power in the universe, which is the power of the Creative Word. As such, this term "heaven" is the combination of spiritual fire and the element of water.

The alchemical symbol of fire is an equilateral triangle with its point upward, and that of water, an equilateral triangle pointing downward. The interlaced triangles have thus become the symbol by which we recognize Solomon's Seal, which is the perfect union of masculine and feminine—Heaven and Earth, above and below, and the principle upon which Solomon's Temple was built. The molecular symbol H_2O is the combination of two ions, the positive electrical, masculine hydrogen ion, combined with the negative, magnetic, feminine oxygen ions, which constitutes water. Chemically, hydrogen is the spirit and universal element; and liquid oxygen has the strongly magnetic quality of matter, so we see that even ordinary water is a compound, which has the characteristic qualities of the alchemical sun, and the alchemical moon.

Though God transcends all distinctions of gender, the actual working power, which is the essence of the dark void of primordial humanity has always been represented by the feminine. The symbol for this feminine power has always been the downward pointed equilateral triangle as it has also always been for both the Greek symbol for Delta and the planet Venus. Sages say that Fire and Water describe this One Thing, the Prima Materia, providing confirmation that the One Life is neither masculine nor feminine, but, in fact, both. We are told in the *Emerald Tablet of Hermes*, that when the One Thing turned into Earth, it expresses as Water, but when it ascends from Earth to Heaven it expresses as Fire, and not as two separate realities. All our sages agree that this water, which is the mother of all *figurable* things, and whose correspondence is the masculine indwelling Fire, is no ordinary Water, but is in fact Alchemical Water. Paracelsus, therefore, declares that the ultimate and primal matter of everything is Fire; that Fire is the key that locks the chest containing those things that are concealed, and that Fire makes visible whatever is hidden in anything.

Furthermore, Alchemical Fire is the Alchemical Water turned into Earth, and through the process of congelation, this heavenly water is the essence from which Earth is formed. Alchemical Water has the fundamental nature of light, and is considered to be, one of the two luminaries, thereby making the sun a likeness of the moon. This heavenly water has been identified as that current of energy whose movement in the agency of manifestation, is seen in the forms of the sun, the moon and the stars.

Alchemical Water is the substance out of which the Earth came into being and, it is that over which the Spirit of God moved, giving birth to everything celestial and terrestrial. This is not the water drawn out of seas, rivers, lakes and fountains but one that has within it all the elements necessary to bring about the perfection of the philosophical work, or Great Work, without any extrinsic additions. It has also been described as being *tortured* or *twisted*, through its spiraling motion, which is essential to the process of the creation of substance. The spiraling motion of this Alchemical Water brings about an alteration within the individual form. The nature and composition of this Divine water is constituted to ensure that through the processes of Man's journey into form and/ or his ascent out of form, he would have within his being, all that is needed to bring him into full conscious remembrance of his Divinity. Thus, it is important to know that the purpose for which humanity entered into form is to have an extended and expanded knowledge of himself, and in this way, with life in general.

The classification and distinction of water above the firmament, and water below the firmament marked out some significant differences in the understanding of the purpose and the goal of involution and evolution. Water below the firmament is considered to be water of death, and an imperfect reflection of the water above the firmament, which is viewed as the water of life. This living water is that which God in Christ has instituted for the baptism of regeneration.[2] Though water is separated out, from fire, they remain linked together, just as the body is linked to the soul. This Alchemical Water, the first element spoken of in Genesis, is the most ancient of principles, and the Mother of all things in manifestation. It is only through this Creative Mother Principle that the Earth can receive any blessing, because moisture is the proper cause of mixture and fusion. The first matter of all minerals is water, which is comprised of Sulphur, Salt, and Mercury. These three are essentially the spirit of all elements, and confirms the alchemical declaration that: "*water is the seed, and root of all metals, and all metals are in fact mineral water*". Alchemical Fire is the activity or Sulphur aspect of the One Reality, while Alchemical Water is the substance or Salt aspect, and Mercury is Alchemical Air—the reconciling aspect between the two. We must keep in mind, however, that this Alchemical Water is not exactly the same as ordinary H_2O; it is in fact hyperphysical or heavenly water in its nature, imbued with the Divine essence which gives rise to all the manifestations that appear in the physical dimension.

Sages report that the Spirit of God has incubated this mystical primordial substance called heavenly water; and it is this spirit, which gives life to that which is dead. The Alchemical Fire is the metaphysical substance of the *archetypal world,* while Alchemical Water is the metaphysical substance of the creative world. Alchemists claim that the primordial substance is said to contain within itself the essence of all that Man is made of. It not only has all the element of the physical being, but more importantly, it has the *breath of life* itself, in a latent state, ready to be awakened. Esoterically, it is at the sound of the trumpet, that the spiritually asleep or dead will awaken to spiritual life. The incubation of the Spirit of God in the being of the individual brings about the *second birth* into full consciousness, and in returning to Oneness with the Father, the individual thus becomes holy, just and wise.[3] It is under the agency of Alchemical Water, that the rule or administration of the Life power, and the conditions of that administration are established over the building and construction of all forms. This in turn makes it possible for the individual, and the aspirant to be restored to his knowledge of being royal, king, and ruler.

For creation to occur the stillness and purity of the Oneness had to be disturbed, thus producing chaos; and, it is through this process that the One sacrificed itself to bring about manifestation. The process of creation, of necessity, required the imposition of limitation, order and measurement, and it is this severe, restricting force that humanity senses as pain and sorrow. On the reverse path of evolution, as the aspirant experiences the expanding influences of that force he then understands the need for the applied force of severity.

The One Life created water as the first matter in nature. Although so soft and seemingly weak, it yields fruit, metal, and stone, which range from the softest to the hardest substances in form. Stability, soundness, vitality, coherence, and solidity: these are the qualities of permanence and substance used to describe Alchemical Water.[4]

Solution is the process through which any substance is absorbed into and homogenously mixed with a liquid, creating an *alchemical-like*, ordinary water, with the ability to dissolve substances as well as to hold them in suspension. This process describes what we call dissolution or death—a process said by adepts to be the great secret of the alchemical operation. It is the secret that the Moon Goddess or High Priestess, conceals in the Book of Law, and which she is now in the process of revealing.

Through dissolution, which is primarily a psychological process, Alchemical Water, the fluid substance we call mind-stuff, lifts the energy stored in the reservoirs of subconsciousness up into the field of conscious awareness. It reveals the secrets that the High Priestess has concealed on her scroll, or Book of Life, and gives the aspirant direct experience of the inner and true nature of all things. It affects changes in the physical and subtle bodies, transforming the vehicle of the aspirant, so that he is able to more perfectly express the Divine idea he was created to make manifest.

These changes, which lead to the achievement of the Great Work, are a result of occult meditation or alchemical solution, and can only be accomplished under the guidance of the *Inner Teacher*, during which process the currents in the regenerative, reproductive Scorpio region of the body, must be disturbed, and reversed. The aspirant is re-oriented and all that is hidden is brought to the surface, through his experience of the tests, trials and the *sting of life*.[5]

Man IS the object of alchemical study and the Great Work. Through study, he discovers that HE is the First Matter of the Philosopher's Stone. Through the alchemical solution, he discovers an absolute identity with this special water, which is identical to the essence of his own being and essential nature. He discovers that his essential nature is also the innermost essence of all things.

Alchemy is defined as: "the universal art of vital chemistry, which by fermenting the human spirit, purifies it, and by finally dissolving it, opens the elementary germ into the new life, and consciousness." The Philosopher's Stone is the outflow or emanation of such a life, drawn to a focus, and made manifest as a concrete Essence of Light. This essence is the true Form or Idea of Gold, and the process takes place in, and through the blood, changing the relation of its component parts and principles.[6] Simultaneously, others declare that alchemy is a science, an art and the philosophy of fire, consisting primarily of the movement and direction of the element of fire which destroys all imperfection and is the active principle or father of separation. The sages warn that if the aspirant is ignorant of the degrees and points of external fire, he should not embark on the Philosophic Work, for he will never obtain light out of darkness. They are both correct, because fire is water, and water is fire, both being aspects of the One Thing.

Through the process of alchemy, the physical, emotional and mental poisons which affect the brain, nerves and ductless or endocrine glands are drawn out of the bodies. These poisons are responsible for serious alterations in the personal character of the individual, which express as silly eccentricities, different phases of emotional instability, profound neuroses, and insanity. It is therefore imperative that the *gross work* be undertaken before any individual undertakes the subtle work of the alchemical process. First Matter is, like the Phoenix, incombustible. It cannot be destroyed by fire, because its inner nature and essence is that of fire. In its whirling, circulating motion, it dances through our veins, moving more slowly through the lymphatic vessels, but rapidly gyrating through the nervous system. This mysterious substance with its spiraling, whirling motion is in the blood and is described as the oiliness of the earth, which refers to the principle of fertility. It is a mineral, yet it is neither mineral nor metal. It is a stone and yet no stone. This is so because it is not restricted to any of these forms. And when the First Matter is brought by the individual to a state of perfection, it is called the Philosophers' Stone or the Universal Medicine.[7]

The River Jordan is associated in biblical scriptures with the bloodstream and to the "Blood of the Lamb", or the Blood of the Christ, which have great esoteric significance especially with regard to the transformation of the individual. Jesus is the elder brother of the race of Man, the man from *Bethlehem*, who walked the path of illumination as a Way-Shower and Guide, and it is interesting to note here that *Bethlehem* is known to Qabalists as the *House of Bread*. Jesus whose purpose was to show Man what he could achieve called himself the *vine,* and at the last supper he referred to the cup as containing his blood. Bread therefore became the support for the physical Man, and blood the support for the spiritual Man, thus providing support for the body and soul. The blood is central to this process of illumination since inner enlightenment is the conversion of energy drawn directly from our daystar, the physical Sun and center of our solar system. This process is not purely a spiritual or mental one, but also a physiological one, involving the alchemical processes in both the blood and the brain. Light alters the function and structure of the cells, and change in the body due to the release of alchemical fire and thus consciousness in the blood, results in modifications to the fabric of the body. These modifications produce refinements, thus providing a greater opportunity for the expression of subtle impulses from the soul.[8]

The element of water is the mother, seed, and root of all minerals. It is the generative potency representing the union of the Father and the Mother, male and female, whereas the blood is the consequence of the union of spirit and water. Biblical scriptures assure us that the Spirit, the Water, and the Blood bear witness on earth, and these three agree in One. The Life is in the blood. And while form comes from water, the blood manifests in the *ascending* scale of the evolution of forms.[9]

Alchemical Water, ultimately, is the cosmic fire, epitomized in the nerve currents and chemistry of the blood stream. Therefore, the purification of this water must be the first work of the alchemist or aspirant. He must chose true foods, regulate his eating habits, control his sex-life, and experience proper kidney elimination. He must learn bit by bit to rebuild his body, sacrificing everything that clouds the life's transparency to the light of the life-power. And finally, he must impose a pattern of the New Image onto his cells through subconscious re-programming.

In the end, after the Spirit of God moves upon the face of the waters, and the ordered lawful activity of the Great Mother completes her work of body-building under the impulse of desire, the cosmic incarnation is brought to a close, and the occult *drying up* or absorption of the sea, as spoken of in the Christian Bible, will become a reality. This drying up is reflected in the interpretation of the sex impulse, macrocosmically and microscopically, which results in the cessation of desire. The direction of alchemical fire to the throat center, instead of to the generative organs occurs, and the withdrawal of the central energy out of responsive form takes place, producing obscuration, and an absorption back into Unity, which characterizes the Path of Return.[10]

Chapter Five

THE SEVEN ASPECTS OF THE FEMININE

We find Seven especial properties in nature whereby this only Mother works
All things...
These are the seven forms of the Mother of all Beings from whence all that is
In this world is generated.

The Secret Doctrine vol. II, H. P. Blavatsky, pg. 634

CHAPTER FIVE

The Seven Aspects
of the Feminine

When the One Life turned into Earth, She established the Kingdom in Matter. The Mother created the seven principles to bring order out of the chaos resulting from the separation out of Unity.

The Seven Sisters of the Pleiades are the wives to the seven Rishis of the Great Bear. They are also the representatives of the seven principles, and the seven Spirits before the throne of God mentioned in the Christian Bible: six being revealed, and one hidden. These seven spirits correspond to the seven sacred planets in order to express Divine life upon the Earth, (which is a non-sacred planet), and to bring about the spiritualization of matter. The seven Rishis are the positive focal points for the seven major cosmic energies, providing the positive pole for the negative pole of the seven wives, who are expressions of the dualism as manifested in their relation to the seven Rishis.[1] Like the seven rays of the Sun, these seven vibrations and forces of energy are expressed on the plane of matter, first, as a triangle of fire, and then as a square, resulting in the septenary nature of Man: The seven planets in the Solar System, the Seven Councils, the seven Governors, the seven days of the weeks, the seven notes in the musical scale, the seven planetary centers of energies or chakras in the body, the seven Paths; the seven initiations and their seven sub-levels or forty-nine levels, all play a role in the regeneration of the human personality.

Man, according to Ageless Wisdom, is a sevenfold, or septenate being. His nature has seven aspects, and can be examined from the perspective of seven different points of view, or principles. He must be viewed as Spirit, and as a spark of the Divine, who is clothed in a garment of flesh, with the goal of growing into the "likeness" of the "Father", of whom he, at present, is an imperfect reflection. This sevenfold nature of Man can be divided into two areas; one containing the three higher principles, called the Triad, the deathless aspect of Man's nature; and the other containing the four lower principles, the Quaternary or the mortal aspect of Man we call the body. Speaking loosely, Man is a composite of Spirit or Soul, and body.[2] The control of form through the septenate energies is an unalterable rule in the inner government of our universe and our particular solar system, as well as in the individual man.[3]

Let us now take a look at all of these to see how the Grand Architect of the Universe put in place systems within systems in an effort to carry out the Divine Plan, a plan that she and her consort, the Divine Masculine, hold together on the Causal Plane.

The Seven Hermetic Principles

These Principles have been handed down through oral tradition over hundreds of centuries from the Master of Masters, the Thrice Great Hermes Trismegistus, and they represent the foundational premise on which the Divine Mother established the Kingdom of Earth. They are:

1. ***The Principle of Mentalism**, states*: "*The ALL is MIND; the Universe is Mental.*" This principle holds that the ALL, or the One Life, is the substantial Reality underlying all things in outward manifestation, which we call the material universe, the phenomenon of Life; and all that is apparent to our material senses is Spirit. As such, the phenomenal world or universe is simply a mental creation of the ALL.[4]

2. ***The Principle of Correspondence**, states: "As above, so below; as below, so above.*" Once grasped, this principle gives the individual the means of solving many dark paradoxes and hidden secrets of nature. There are many planes beyond the level of the average Man's knowing, but when the principle of correspondence is applied, he is able to understand much that otherwise would be unknowable.[5]

3. ***The Principle of Vibration**, states: "Nothing rests; everything vibrates.*" This principle explains that, the differences between manifestations of matter, energy, mind, and even Spirit are the result of varying rates of vibration, and it embodies the fact that everything is in motion, everything vibrates and nothing rests— a fact now endorsed by modern science.[6]

4. ***The Principle of Polarity**, states: "Everything is dual; everything has poles; everything has its pair of opposites; like*

and unlike are the same; opposites are identical in nature, but different in degree; extremes meet; all truths are but half-truths; all paradoxes may be reconciled." A radical and extreme example of this principle is "Love and Hate", two mental states that seem apparently totally different; yet there are degrees of Love and Hate, and a middle point where we use the terms "like", and "dislike", which shades into each other so gradually that it can be difficult to know where like and dislike begin and end.[7]

5. *The Principle of Rhythm*: *"Everything flows, out and in; everything has its tides; all things rise and fall; the pendulum-swing manifests in everything; the measure of the swing to the right is the measure of the swing to the left; rhythm compensates."* This principle embodies the truth that there is always an action and a reaction, an advance and retreat, a rising and a sinking; and that this holds true in the affairs of the Universe, the suns, the worlds, men, animals, mind, energy and matter. This law is manifested in the creation and the destruction of worlds, in the rise and fall of nations, in the life of all things, and most importantly in the mental state of Man.[8]

6. *The Principle of Cause and Effect*: *"Every Cause has its effect; every Effect has its Cause; everything happens according to Law; Chance is but a name for Law not recognized; there are many planes of causation; but nothing escapes the Law."* In other words, nothing ever "merely happens", and that there is no such thing as Chance, but that while there are various planes of Cause and Effect, with the higher dominating the lower planes, nothing ever entirely escapes the Law.[9]

7. ***The Principle of Gender***: *"Gender is in everything; everything has its Masculine and Feminine Principles; Gender manifests on all planes."* On the physical plane, this principle manifests as the sexes, but on the higher planes it takes higher forms. The principle of Gender always works in the direction of generation, regeneration and creation. Everything and every person contains these two elements. Every Male thing has the Female Element, and every Female contains the Male Principle.[10]

Spirit is the active, conditioning element within every life form. It is the agent responsible for whatever form life takes as it expresses on the plane of matter, for without Spirit nothing exists. All manifestations on this plane is controlled by seven great spirits through the dispersal of their invisible essences, and these seven spirits correspond to the seven planets described below:

The Seven Spirits Correspond to the Seven Planets as described below:

1. Sun, whose attending angel is Michael, is related to the metal gold, to the heart center; and to Sunday

2. Moon, whose attending angel is Gabriel, is related to the metal silver, to the pituitary gland; and to Monday.

3. Mars, whose attending angel is Kamael, is related to the metal iron, to the center below the navel; and to Tuesday.

4. Mercury, whose angel is Raphael, is related to the metal quicksilver, to the cerebrum and pineal body; and to Wednesday

5. Jupiter, whose attending angel is Tzadkiel, is related to the metal tin, to the solar plexus; and to Thursday.

6. Venus, whose attending angel is Anael, is related to the metal copper, to the throat center in the body, and to Friday.

7. Saturn, whose attending angel is Tsaphkiel, is related to the metal lead, to the center at the base of the spine; and to Saturday.[11]

Keeping in mind that all things came into manifestation to have an experience in matter, Man 'died to life above', to be resurrected to life on Earth, and once attaining full consciousness, is then able to return home. To obtain that objective, vehicles or bodies must be appropriately and precisely constructed to allow for eventual regeneration and to be able to be liberated from the bondage that matter first imposes. As we examine all these sepentary influences on all manifested forms, we must consider the perpetual influence of the Mother, whether she appears in a masculine or feminine expression. The seven planetary systems of our solar system, which operated through the seven planetary systems of the planet Earth, as well as in the human body are referred to as charkas and are conduits through which the Cosmic Forces of the Universe are conditioned for development, according to the Divine plan.

The planet *Venus* is more widely associated with the Mother, and we will now reveal her inner nature to explain why her function is essential to the plan. Venus is considered to be pure love and wisdom, and descends to Earth in order to condition the mind and heart by facilitating the generation of the Christ Principle into matter. Venus and Virgo, the virgin mother, represent two aspects of intelligence. These two together with Mercury and other planets play a critical role in influencing the mental linkages necessary for the unfoldment of consciousness in the individual.

The stages of that mental unfoldment are: instinct, intellect, intuition, illumination, inspiration, and finally identification. As the individual develops, Venus reveals the desire of the pairs of opposite for each other, which is, in fact, the underlying theme of the entire creative and evolutionary process. Venus also reveals to Man the desire for the whole, for the universal, and the significant result of the *desire* that urged him to take form on the plane of matter. As Man learns how to transmute knowledge into wisdom, Her role is to emphasize that the Son of God, who is also the Sun of Mind, is the instrument of God's love. She awakens the sense of duality in humanity, which is the underlying factor in the conflict between Desire and Spiritual Will. The exoteric influence of Venus and Libra, allows the individual to recognize his "enemy", and to forge friendships and unions; and it is Venus who links Man-to-Man, and nation-to-nation.[12]

The Venus center in the body —the nerve plexus in man's throat, is the link between the four lower centers in the body and the two higher centers in the head. Alchemists say the sun rises from the heart, through the Venus center, to be joined to the Moon, the pituitary gland. Through the sun center, located in the cardiac plexus in the upper trunk, the physical organism receives what alchemical philosophers would call undifferentiated radiant energy or Prana, which originates in the physical sun in the sky. The radiant energy in the heart is the counterpart to the radiant energy of the physical sun, and cannot remain in the body, but must rise to the head to be combined with the forces emanating from the center of the Moon or pituitary center, and the Mercury or pineal center. The rise of this solar force to the Venus center awakens the function of the Venus center and the state of consciousness produced is predominantly emotional, thus stirring desire into intense activity, since very little progress in practical occult development can be achieved by purely intellectual curiosity. No one can really *know* unless he is also able to *feel*, since the inner door must open toward the heart rather than toward the head. While this initiates the process of spiritual awakening, later on the same door must swing the other way, to allow the force from the heart center to rise through the throat in order to enter and energize the brain. Every aspirant will come to realize the deep level of physiological adjustments needed as a strong body and sound mind are essential to success in the work of conscious regeneration.[13]

Qabalists assign the Hebrew letter Daleth, which means "the door" to Venus, and is the fourteenth of the thirty-two paths of wisdom, referred to as Luminous Intelligence, and the "institutor of arcane." She is not so much the door, as she is the "valve" to the door, or the bar to the entrance and she ultimately becomes the barrier to the aspirant's entrance into the secret place at the center, where the Great Treasure is hidden. To pass through this barrier and to open the "door" is to clear the way to the adytum of god-nourished silence; but this door, which leads to the understanding of the mathematical and psychological principles at work in the construction of the universe, is only open to the perfected consciousness of the illuminated Man.[14]

Mercury is considered the star of conflict, and is the major planet of relationships because it governs and engineers the interplay with our planet, Earth, through the conditioning constellations of Aries and Gemini.[15] Mercury is the messenger of the Gods to Man, revealing the Spiritual Trinity to the soul of the aspirant as he takes his steps on the path of initiation. Mercury works with Venus, who conditions the inner work of the individual to elicit the embryonic understanding of causes and conditions to complete this task. It is Mercury that conditions the mind toward the will-to-be, which initiated the beginning of Man's incarnation upon the Earth, as well as the idea to be in form. This same *force of will* influences the idea to initiate all new decisions, including freedom from form.

As the Divine messenger, the Principle of Illusion, and the Expression of the active Higher mind, one of Mercury's missions is to lead humanity into light, to lead the Christ-child out of the womb of time and flesh into the light of day and of manifestation; in order to accomplish the task of establishing humanity as a center of power on the Earth.[16]

The fluid nature of Mercury allows it to be the mediator and reconciler of many forces, because it signifies the versatile energy of the Son/Sun of Mind, the soul; it is interchangeable for Sun (Son) and stands for the mediator or intermediary between the Father and the Mother, between Spirit and Matter, while at the same time it is the result of the union of these two.[17] Through conflict, Will, Love, and Harmony, are the controlling forces which make Man what he is. These are the governing and directing energies which use Mercury, the mind, together with the emotional and love nature of Jupiter, through the physical form established by the Moon, to satisfactorily bring humanity to its present point of evolution on its probationary path of fire.

As stated in previous chapters, Saturn creates crises in the life of the individual and provides opportunities and choices to bring about needed changes, including the destruction of whatever holds back the free expression of the soul. Eventually, Saturn stands aside to allow His great brother Mercury to spread the illuminating and intuitive light of the soul upon the situation. Then, through our own illumined minds, an understanding of the significance of the events is achieved, and the aspirant is able to relate the old to the new, and the past to the future, through the light of the present.[18] To this end, the present trend to meditation has great subjective usefulness because it *impresses from on high*, and illuminates by the *light of the soul*.

The work of Saturn and Mercury prepares the individual for the work of Venus by establishing the union of heart and mind, as well as ushering in the long awaited era of love, wisdom, brotherhood, and brotherly relationships. Mercury rules the hands and the lungs, and to achieve completion of the Great Work, which is performed with the aid of Mercury, manual operation involving fine workmanship, great dexterity and a sense of touch is essential. The following rule reveals much about Mercury, the messenger:

Let the disciple learn the use of the hand in service
Let him seek the mark of the messenger in his feet, and
Let him learn to see with the eye that looks out from between the two.

From an occult standpoint the *use of the hands,* is the utilization of the chakra centers in the hand, for healing bodily ills; curing emotional ills, raised in prayer or for in manipulating the mental currents and energy in meditation.

The *mark of the messenger* alludes to the well-known symbol of the wings on the heel of Mercury. The expression, *the eye, which looks out from between the two,* speaks to the inner vision of that which all self-consciousness develops, and to the Higher Self or Spirit, which looks out through the two eyes of the little self.[19]

The *Moon,* the mother of forms, is the symbol of matter, and deals with *the lunar mansions,* the home of the soul in all three worlds of human endeavor. Greater knowledge of the lunar forms reveals an understanding of the physical body, the astral vehicle, and the mental sheath. And as the aspirant focuses his concentration on the moon, it will reveal its nature and purpose. On the contrary, the Sun in its aspects of light, is the symbol of the soul and deals with the various states of consciousness, while the moon deals with the vehicle of consciousness, the body incorruptible, not made with hands and eternal in the heavens.[20]

The Moon, and the moon center in the body, the pituitary gland, are concerned with the exoteric influences, which affect the ordinary life of the human, bringing about the fusion of the will-to-be and to know, and of the heart and mind, which leads to the inclination in the aspirant to create the conditions that lead to the significant and critical transformations of instinct into intellect. The Moon is said by sages to veil the mysterious and occult planet Uranus, and now that this veil is being removed, this ruler of the Aquarian Age is causing great transference in the human consciousness from intellectual perceptions to intuitive knowledge. These influences are now producing the conditions necessary to help the soul express more freely, and to develop into a leader. Water, the symbol of substance and material expression including emotional motivation, is conditioned by the forces of Uranus, which effect changes in the blood and bring the individual to a higher turn on the wheel, in the Age of Aquarius. Now his nature is determined, his qualities are fixed, and these deeper influences and potencies will motive his activities.[21]

The function of the Moon has always been to create the appropriate vehicle for the soul, to dwell in and to prepare it for the final initiation. At this stage, the Moon has completed its obligation and ceases to be, since Uranus, which it had veiled, is now dominant.

Qabalists assign the High Priestess to the Moon, and the thirteenth path on the Tree of Life, and the Hebrew name, Gimel, meaning *Camel*, the animal/ship of the desert. She, the High Priestess, is said to be the keeper of the occults secrets of life and of the law on which the foundations of the world is built. She represents the element of water and is the basis on which the Life Power has grounded its perfect remembrance of all it has ever done. This perfect memory held by the High Priestess is none other than that of the One Identity, which links and unites all personalities. Every human being has access to this imperishable and perfect record of the past that she keeps. She is the Uniting Intelligence, and just as the symbol of the *Camel* is associated with transportation and commerce, she unites one point in space with another and carries news from one place to another.

The *thirteenth path* of the thirty-two paths of wisdom, to which she is assigned, gives her the designation of Chief Female Elder of the Temple. She sits with the scroll in her lap, on the porch of Solomon's Temple between two pillars, one black, and one white, to draw attention to the pairs of opposites, and to be the reconciler of both. The thirteenth path conveys to every Qabalist the combined ideas of Unity and Love, which are associated with the number thirteen. And, as all love, is typified by the Woman, who is the object of love, there is a powerful connection between this thirteenth path and the many feminine aspects of the One Life. The thirteenth path begins in the sphere of Tiphareth, the Sun/Son and Christed Being and the Teacher, and leads the aspirant up the long path that eventually takes him back to Kether, the Father's House. To walk this path, one must have a full comprehension of the principles of cyclic motion, which are exemplified in astronomy. The principle of cyclic motion is fundamental in the cosmos and in Ageless Wisdom, which teaches that the same force that keeps the stars in place, is manifest in all activity everywhere.[22] Mankind "draws nigh" to the Father through the process of recollection, by unrolling the scroll of memory, which the High Priestess holds in her lap, and in doing so, we unite ourselves to the One Life. The Book of Books, spoken of in the Book of Revelation, is none other than the scroll of the High Priestess, made of lambskin and sealed with seven seals. These secrets are never written, nor are they communicated in the words of any human tongue. This mysterious document of arcane wisdom, which it has taken God eons to write, is a Bible, and when rightly read, it discloses cosmic mysteries. It is in fact the human body, and its seals are the seven charkas or radiant forces of energy proclaiming the words of the Logos. These seals are the same as the seven societies and the seven lamp-stands; and, the expression "written inside and on the back" refers to the cerebro-spinal axis, and the great sympathetic system.[23] During his further translation of the Apocalypse Mr. Pyrse, in alluding to his book, writes: "And I saw a strong Divinity proclaiming with a great voice: "Who is worthy to open the scroll and force it open." He goes on to say that the "strong Divinity is none other than Kronos, the God of Time, who is also Saturn."[24]

The thirty-second, and final path of wisdom, on the Tree of Life, is that of *Saturn.* In the *Book of Formation*, Saturn is called the Administrative, or Assisting Intelligence, because it directs all operations of the seven planets, and all their divisions.

Saturn is the symbol of the Universe, an orderly, rhythmic manifestation of life, determined by fixed laws. It is the astrological symbol of all that makes things solid, definite and concrete. These are the reasons why Saturn is regarded as malefic. Its role is to set boundaries and limits in order to create a prescribed field of operation for working out the events of one's life.

"Dominion and Slavery", is the pair of opposites representing the path of Saturn, and Man is a co-creator, who shares in the administration of the Great Work, and assists in the evolution of the Great Plan for the liberation of humanity. Humanity is in servitude when he operates as one who is asleep, blind, and operating as a part of a herded mass of men-animal who is hardly aware of being alive. However, when He unfolds his own consciousness, functions with his eyes opened, and in full awareness of what is happening around him, He shares consciously in the Cosmic Administration and Dominion of all things.[25]

Kingsford and Maitland, in *The Perfect Way*, refer to Satan as the keeper of the keys to the Sanctuary, and makes plain that occultists know that in the classification of systems and of types in Ageless Wisdom, Saturn and Satan are closely connected. They further state:

> And on the Seventh Day, there went forth from the presence of God a mighty Angel, full of wrath and consuming fire, and God gave unto him the dominion of the outermost sphere. Eternity brought forth Time; the Boundless gave birth to Limit; Being descended into Generation. As lightning I beheld Satan fall from heaven, splendid in strength and fury. Among the Gods is none like unto him, into whose hand are committed the kingdoms, the power and the glory of the world.
> Blessed are they who shall withstand his subtlety: they shall be called the sons of God, and shall enter in at the beautiful gates. For Satan is the doorkeeper of the Temple of the King: he standeth in Solomon's porch;

he holdeth the Keys of the Sanctuary; that no Man may enter therein save the anointed, having the Arcanum of Hermes.[26]

Saturn is called the Lord of Karma and the imposer of retribution, as well as the one who demands full payment of all debts, and therefore condemns Man to the struggle of existence, both from the form and soul sides of life. Saturn's influence ends however when his work is accomplished, and this occurs when Spiritual Man has freed himself through *acquiescence* and *aspiration* and the conscious effects of the completed cycle of the four energies of matter he was subjected to from the power of the Mutable Cross. He has also freed himself from a veiled vision and incipient longing of the goal of the Fixed Cross where he now becomes illumined by understanding the purpose of the Mutable Cross. Saturn cannot follow, and will not follow, the liberated man to the Cardinal Cross, because Saturn's work is now complete.

In the Age of Aquarius, Saturn will have three important functions:

1. Saturn will serve to produce a dividing of the ways and a proffering of opportunity to those who can avail themselves of it. There will, therefore, be a period of discipline, and a cycle where choices will be made, and through these discriminating decisions, humanity will enter into its birthright.

2. Saturn, in conjunction with Mercury, who pours in the light of mental and spiritual illumination, and a truer interpretation of the teachings of the Lodge of Messengers, will facilitate humanity in making the choices that will

enable Man to raise the lower energies into the higher centers above the diaphragm, thereby bringing about a fusing of the personality and the soul, and the birth of the Christ within him.

3. Venus and Saturn will inaugurate the rule of Brotherhood, with Venus' controlling intelligent love so that the group, not the individual, will be the important unit, and unselfishness and cooperation will steadily take the place of separativeness and competition.[27]

The polar opposite of the planet Saturn, the planet of limitation and restriction, is the planet *Jupiter,* which is known as the planet of expansion and is. The Saturn force is the spiral moving towards the center with a contracting energy, while the Jupiter force, also a spiral, moves away from the center and diffuses energy. Its influence indicates that the way of incarnation is the most *beneficent* method of evolutionary unfoldment, and that the way of love-wisdom is the way for humanity to go. The work of Jupiter is to develop in every human being the connection between the head and the heart, between mind and love, between will and wisdom, thus bringing these two qualities into synthetic interplay.[28] The fusion of heart and mind is the subjective purpose for which life was manifested on our planet, and so Jupiter provides the inherent tendency to fusion which nothing can arrest. When the human family is fully awakened to spiritual, as opposed to material possibilities, then the work of Jupiter will immediately intensify, and this beneficent ruler will lead humanity into the ways of peace and progress.[29]

Jupiter is also the deity known as the symbol and prototype of ritualistic worship—the personification of cyclic law—and together with Saturn, they preside over "The Mysteries". Jupiter is the priest, the sacrificer, the suppliant and the medium through which the prayers of mortals reach to the Gods. The sign of the Messiah's coming is the conjunction of Jupiter and Saturn in the sign of Pisces.[30] This planet of beneficence represents the fourth sphere on the Tree of Life called Mercy, Measuring, and Arresting. Arresting, because it rises like a boundary to receive the emanations of the higher intelligences pouring down from the Supreme Crown, Kether, as expressed through the Father, Chokmah, and the Mother, Binah, on the Tree of Life. The solar plexus is where the Jupiter force resides in the body, and this is the organ of our psychological rapport with other human beings as well as the occult center of our contact with the memory of the lower kingdoms.

Jupiter, the ruler and conveyor of expansion, significantly expresses itself to bring the individual to ripeness in the three worlds of human evolution, through the four signs of Virgo, Pisces, Sagittarius and Aquarius, which represent four different elements.

- In the sign of the Virgin Mother, Virgo, a mutable Earth sign, the Hidden Christ is nurtured
- In the mutable Water sign of Pisces, Jupiter brings forth the Hidden Savior
- In the mutable Fire sign of Sagittarius, the Hidden Master is brought to the world
- In the Fixed Air sign of Aquarius, the Hidden World server is given to the world.

Mars is the planetary force that rules, conditions, and controls the entire physical vehicle called the personality. This planet is not malefic, as many tend to believe, and while it is this fiery energy that propelled life into manifestation, at the same time, Mars is the God of war, destruction, change, and death. The influences of Mars lead to idealism, destructive fanaticism, struggle, strife, and war, which were the characteristics of the Age of Pisces that has just ended. Unfortunately, there are many who are desperately holding on to that past—a past, which cannot be recaptured. Mars is the primary ruler of both Aries and Scorpio. Aries is the 'the birthplace of divine ideas.' These can be the ideas a soul brings into incarnation, and are controlled by Mars until that soul is re-oriented and as it matures, becomes sensitive to the influence of Mercury. On the other hand those Divine ideas may also be the birth of the ideas of the Divine Plan, to which the Initiate becomes sensitive. Aries is one of the three signs in which the representative animals have horns; the other two being the Bull in Taurus and the Goat in Capricorn. The downward turn of the Ram's horns in Aries signifies the coming into manifestation and the involutionary cycle of the Divine idea initiated by Aries. Aries should also be recognized as the Divine Manifestation, which Christ referred to when he said: "I am the Alpha and the Omega, the beginning and the end." This will be a reality in the Age of Aquarius, when Aries, the first sign of the zodiac fuse with Pieces, the last sign of the zodiac, to become one sign. Aries governs the Path to Discipleship, the Will to return to the Source, and the determination to achieve liberation. The Ram leads humanity into the creative life on Earth, into the darkness of matter, and. when that experience is complete, the door will open into the Father's House. Aries then, is the focal point of expression of the first aspect of divinity, the aspect of Will associated with the Father's House and the Great Bear and especially with one of the stars called The Pointers, which points to the Pole Star, "the star of direction"; a star signifying the direction, purpose, and plan of the Father.[31]

The Tower of Babel, a structure constructed to reinforce separateness and to give permanency and security to form, symbolizes Mars in Qabalah. However, Ageless Wisdom does not support this illusionary notion, but states that no form is permanent, nor does any form separate a portion of the One Identity from the whole of that Identity. The Reality manifested at any point in space, is identical to the Reality that exists at all points of space. And is the same Reality that existed in the past, that exist in the present, and that will exist in the future.[32] On the involutionary journey initiated by Aries, Man entered into separation, illusion, and erroneous thinking and lived out this distorted reality, until he is met, face to face, by the Father on the Return Path. The effect of Mars is massive, and produces great struggles, which finally lead to great revelations. In Aries, that revelation is— the nature of knowledge, and the purpose of incarnation. Mars influence is in the sign of Scorpio, which it rules. Mankind reverses his path when his illusionary experience with matter is completed, and in Scorpio, the sign of death, Mars brings about a crisis of the soul, and reveals the vision of liberation and service to the aspirant. The connection between Mars and the blood, as well as the fire in the blood sets up the eternal conflict between life and death. It does this through its influence on the Scorpio center, the reproductive center below the navel. In Scorpio, Mars inflicts the "sting of the Scorpion", with its influence bringing about a death to the previous life of the candidate for Initiation. The tests of duality applied by Mars enables the aspirant to pass through the second doorway of initiation and demonstrate that the desire nature is subdued, and the lower nature is conquered.

The lower sexual nature is lifted up "into heaven", so that the initiate will be fit for service in Aquarius.[33]

It is under the sign of Scorpio, that the Prodigal Son who wandered from home and heritage, leaves the limitations of the five-sense life, and makes the journey back to the Holy Land.[34] The Sun stands for life of the Spirit, and is that which comes into full expression in the aspirant as a result of the urge to return in Scorpio, this urge is initiated by Aries in which the Sun is exalted.

The triple nature of the *Sun,* like the Trinity, will become known to Man, as he traverses the twelve divisions of life we call the zodiac. And at the appropriate time, his soul will reveal to him its true nature. These three aspects of the Sun—the Physical Sun, the Heart Sun, and the Central Spiritual Sun—are the factors, which initiate the birthing of consciousness making the ultimate goal attainable. The Sun makes all forms of consciousness possible. *The Physical Sun* influences the form, or personality of the individual, by conditioning those energies within him that allows for the organization of substance, and the invocation of sensitive responses to substance itself. This awakening of the personality to soul control by the Physical Sun, works through the centers of Saturn and Neptune whose influence in the body is in the seventh center, located at the base of the spine. The Physical Sun catalyses an upward surge of kundalini fire, which fuses with the energies at the top of the head, allowing the aspirant to awaken to the reality of Soul-will, desire, and intent in the physical, emotional and mental worlds.[35] The Physical or Mutable Cross, which represents the third person of the Trinity and the Physical Man, is the Cross on which He is crucified, stimulating the bodily cells and sustaining the form nature, thus affecting the centers below the diaphragm.

An individual's "sun sign" indicates the quality of the individual's physical, mental, spiritual nature. The sun sign holds the secret of the personality ray and the aspirant's responsiveness, or lack thereof, to the Soul. It also indicates the level of integration already achieved, and the present stage of unfoldment of the soul qualities, the present equipment, the present life quality, and the possible immediate group relations.[36]

The Heart Sun, or the Heart of the Sun, influences the heart. Neptune is the agent employed to bring about this activation, once the individual is on the Fixed Cross. The Heart of the Sun, through Neptune, pours its energies upon the aspirant, affecting the heart, the throat, and the *ajna*, which is the center between the eyebrows. Neptune, Diety of the waters, governs the emotional plane of desire, and when this planetary force becomes active in the body, emotion-desire is transmuted into love-aspiration, and re-orients the aspirant to the Soul. On the Fixed Cross, the second person of the Trinity, the Son, is crucified. It is the Son who, driven by love to incarnate in matter, is now to be crucified upon the Cross of Matter. The aspirant upon the Fixed Cross begins to grasp the hierarchical purpose. This can only be grasped by the Man who is willing to be crucified on that Cross. As he reaches the stage of responsibility, self-awareness, and direction, the aspirant's orientation is now "spiritual vertical", which involves the inclusive horizontal, and at this stage, the Divine Plan begins to take shape in his consciousness.[37]

The *Central Spiritual Sun*, the third aspect of the Sun, has its center in the body in the head, and is influenced by the Sun and Sirius. The Central Spiritual Sun directly influences the Man upon the Cardinal Cross, where the purpose and the unified consummations of the crucifixions on the mutable and fixed crosses becomes almost blindly apparent and a vision of the unified intent of the three Persons of the underlying Trinity, each on his own cross, becomes very clear. The sign of Leo represents the element of fire, the Lion, king/queen of the jungle, and is ruled by the Sun, which also rules the heart in the human body. Leo is directly related to Sirius, and the clue or mystery to two great mysteries lies in this sign. The first relates to the mystery of the Sphinx, and is connected with the mystery of the higher and lower minds. As it relates to Leo, Virgo and the solar Angels, the dual development of subjective and objective consciousness results in "the final judgment" where "the Lion and the Virgin", soul and form, are fused to become one sign. At this point, Man's antagonistic dualism becomes complete and the scales will have turned in favor of what the Virgin-Mother has hidden from expression for eons. The second relates to the mystery of the Lion and the Unicorn, which contains the secret of Initiation, and the "going up" of the human entity to the portal of admittance into the Hierarchy, as well as to the "mystic raising" of which Masonry holds the key. This is directly related to the emergence of the initiate's consciousness, and the defeat of the king of beasts (the personality), which leads to the triumph of the group, to world consciousness, and to illumination over self-consciousness, and selfishness. In the ancient myth, the king of beasts is blinded and killed, by the piercing of the eye and heart by the long horn of the unicorn.[38] These three Crosses—the Mutable, Fixed and Cardinal— in their totality of manifestation are related to the three basic energies which brought the solar system into being because they constitute the three major and synthetic expressions of the supernal Will, motivated by love, and expressed through activity.[39]

Qabalah assigns the thirtieth path on the Tree of Life to the Sun, the symbol of the regeneration of the personality of Man, the only one capable of accomplishing the Great Work and bringing it to completion and the particular purpose for which Man was brought into existence. The Hebrew name *Resch* meaning head or face of man is assigned to the Sun as it is in the human head and countenance that the controlling elements of the Life Power are concentrated. This can be summed up thus:

> *Man is the synthesis of all cosmic activities.*
> *Human intelligence gathers together all the*
> *various threads of the Life Power's self-manifestation*
> *and carries that manifestation beyond anything*
> *that could come into existence*
> *apart from Man and human intelligence.*[40]

Liberation from the bondage of ignorance in the three worlds of illusion can only be achieved through perfectly maintained discrimination; and the duality of nature, spirit and matter must first be accepted as a logical basis before any further work can occur. It is mandatory that the aspirant assume the attitude of the higher polarity, which is that of spirit manifesting as the Soul, or inner ruler. As a consequence, it becomes essential for him to discriminate in everyday affairs between the Real Self and the Personality, which is the sum total of the lower manifestation—the physical, emotional, and mental Man. This process of re-thinking and regeneration, of necessity, includes the following seven major modifications:

The Seven Major Modifications of Mind-Consciousness

1. *Desire for knowledge:* A desire for knowledge is what drove the Prodigal Son into the three worlds of illusion; and it is this same urge that sent Spirit into incarnation. This experience in the world of illusion brings the aspirant to the place where he can say "I now know all I need to know." This knowing allows his place on the ladder to be revealed to him, and brings about the first modification in the thinking principle, as it relates to a desire for knowledge.[41]

2. *Desire for freedom:* The result of living through many life cycles brings the aspirant to the place where he longs for a different condition—to be liberated and freed from the cycles of death and rebirth. This stage is long and arduous, but at this stage he frees himself from any limitation, from any fetters that bind him, and can say, "I am free."[42]

3. *Desire for happiness:* This is the basic longing of every human being, and is based on the inherent quality of discrimination. With a deep capacity to contrast his present state with that of the "Father's House", the Prodigal Son remembers that time of satisfaction. This capacity for happiness and bliss produces an urge, dissatisfaction, and a restlessness to return to that former time, which brings about a shift in the consciousness out of the lower personality up to the higher spiritual consciousness, centered in the soul and the Christ nature. With the desire for happiness now satisfied and transcended, the aspirant can now say, "I have now reached my goal, and nothing remains in the three worlds of illusion."[43]

4. *Desire to do one's duty:* Modification, in the above three thinking principles, brings humanity to a state where the

motive for life comes down to the fulfillment of one's duty in life. His longing for knowledge, happiness, and freedom brings him now to a place of total dissatisfaction, because he has exhausted the search for joy for himself. His horizons are now widened, and he awakens to his responsibility and obligations to others and to humanity as a whole. He has fulfilled the Law of Karma, becoming a Master and a wielder of the Law.[44]

5. *Sorrow:* The response of the human vehicle to pain and sorrow increases as he advances upon the ladder of conscious evolution, and the more refined their vehicle, the greater the response of the nervous system to pain and pleasure. His sense of values becomes very acute, and he becomes very sensitive to the suffering of humanity. With complete control of the mind achieved, the seer understands the need for mental development, and the mind finally comes to rest when surrender to the higher mind occurs. Sorrow is dispelled by the glory of illumination. The pairs of opposites are no longer at war.[45]

6. *Fear*: As modifications in the thinking principle become more rapid, and the mental body develops, fears of the mind, based upon memory, imagination, anticipation, and the power to visualize, are very difficult to overcome and can only be achieved by the domination of the Soul. Fear in the aspirant finally gives way to the knowledge that there is nothing in him that can attract evil, death or pain to him. With this comes the realization of the true nature of Divinity, and so utter bliss takes the place of fear.[46]

7. *Doubt:* This relates to causes more than effect. The Man who doubts essentially doubts himself as the arbiter of his

fate. When the aspirant begins to question the capacity of the mind to explain, interpret, and comprehend, he has basically exhausted the sum total of his resources in the three worlds of illusion. At this final stage, doubt no longer controls, and the full light of day or complete illumination takes place and fills the entire body of the seer. The initiate can now say in full conscious knowledge: "I am that I am", as he now knows himself to be one with the All- Self. These are the seven stages on the Path of Return; they are synonymous with the seven stations of the cross of the Christian religion, the seven great initiations, and the seven ways of bliss.[47]

Chapter Six

THE HEART, ITS ROLE
IN CONSCIOUSNESS

*When the Heart of the Body throbs with Spiritual energy, when its
sevenfold content thrills under the spiritual impulse, then the currents
spread and circulate and Divine manifestation becomes a Reality;
the Divine Man incarnates."*
The Old Commentary

CHAPTER SIX
The Heart, It's Role in Consciousness

Anatomically, the heart is described as a hollow, cone-shaped muscular organ about five inches long, three and one-half inches wide, and two and one-half inches thick. Its weight varies from ten to twelve ounces in men and eight to ten ounces in the women, and it is positioned at an angle in the chest, with its apex directed forward, downward and to the left. Divided by a longitudinal muscular septum, and a transverse constriction, it has four cavities— two upper cavities, the auricles, and two lower cavities, the ventricles. In reality, the heart could be considered a double organ because its right side is dedicated to receiving venous or impure blood, which enters the right auricle through the veins, and then passes to the right ventricle where it is taken away from the heart through the pulmonary artery to the lungs to be purified. The blood then returns to the left side of the heart through the pulmonary veins, entering the left auricle, and from there the blood passes to the left ventricle and then leaves the heart via the aorta and its many arteries to supply oxygen and nutrients to the entire body. Dr. Charles W. Chapman indicates that there is a sino-auricular node, a small specialized mass of tissue, situated at the place where the superior vena cave meets the right auricle. This node, said to be the seat of the origin of the heartbeat, is called the pacemaker, and is thought to receive fibers from the vagus and sympathetic nerves.

Philosophers comment that there is an occult significance to the circulation of the blood, and indicate that the blood contains an airy, fiery spirit whose center is in the heart where it is most condensed and from which it radiates out not only to the whole body but also out into the atmosphere, until it returns to the heart. Paracelsus thus establishes a universal correspondence to the similar effect that the fiery spirit of the sun has on the atmosphere of the planetary scheme. An analogy is also made to the world soul in form and function as a center of the supreme principle of intelligence and vitality, since where there is intelligence there must be vitality, and the heart exists in the most precious part of the body. Of all the centers in the body, the heart symbolizes the principle of intelligence and vitality, and Man has his supreme sensation in the blood around the heart.

Philosophers claim that the elements of earth and water, fire and air, and heaven and earth are in Man, and that the planets, the stars, and the Milky Way have their mystical correspondence in his heart. Man, they say, is the living temple of God, and the heart is the Holy of Holies of that temple. It is a Mystery Temple, and microcosmically the palace of the king. This temple was always seen as a symbol of a spiritual universe in the midst of a material one. Just as the temple was at the heart of the cultural life of the community, which supports the well being of Man, so was the heart the support of the physical body. It was for this reason that the heart, with all its Hidden Places, became the pattern on which many temples were constructed, since somewhere in its chambers was the mysterious Hierophant known as the "Master of the Hidden House" that no man has ever seen.[1] In the Mystery schools of Egypt and Greece, among Moslems, Hindus, Jews and Christians, the heart is seen not only as the temple of God, but as the Holy City of Jerusalem, also called the temple or tabernacle below and the house in the center of all. The heart is the chief, king of all the organs of the body and of all the divinities in Man; it therefore receives the highest position in the body and is said to contain the seven correlating centers in the body, which we call charkas. Additionally, the seven churches mentioned in the Book of Revelation, and the seven holy cities are analogous to the *Anahata* chakra, located in the center of the heart. The Hindus liken this chakra to a twelve-petalled vermillion flower, with the masculine upturned triangle, and the downward pointing feminine triangle, in the center. The germ of *Pragna*, located in this chakra is likened to "universal consciousness", and when Man's consciousness is centralized in this germ, a state of ecstasy is realized.[2] The Old Commentary says: "When the Heart of the Body throbs with spiritual energy, and its sevenfold content vibrates under the spiritual impulse, then the currents spread and circulate and Divine manifestation becomes a reality, as the Divine Man is born."[3]

Eastern occultism states that at the time of death, the spirit withdraws its radiations from the parts and extremities of the body to the heart and that point of the heart then becomes luminous as the soul departs. We learn from the sixth Khanda of the Khandogya-Upanishad that there are one hundred and one arteries in the heart, one of which penetrates the crown of the head, and the one hundredth and first artery goes directly to that point in the head where the door of Spirit is located. H. P. Blavatsky states that even if the head is severed from the body, the heart will continue to beat for thirty minutes, and will even beat for hours longer if wrapped in cotton wool and put in a warm place. She further states that this spot in the heart, which is the last to die, is the seat of life, the center of all, and is what the Hindus called Brahma or the Absolute Primordial Essence; this is the first spot that lives in the fetus, and is the last to die. It contains potential mind, life, energy, and will. During life, it is said to radiate the seven prismatic colors, which are opalescent and fiery. The flame in the heart consists of the complete spectrum, revealing that all the seven principles which conspire to precipitate the objective Man, have their thrones and spiritual existence in the greater spirit of the whole undifferentiated spiritual life of the Man. Consequently, there are seven brains in the heart, and seven hearts in the brain. The seven brains in the heart are the intelligences of the vital organs. All things physical are the manifestation of Spirit in matter, so the Seven Spirits before the Throne of God, as stated in the previous chapter, do not actually leave the *face* of their Lord, but it is rather their reflections that are visible as is the case regarding the Planetary Lords of the Solar System. These Seven Logi or Cosmic Lords are all in the Sun. A study of the Qabalah will reveal an understanding of how their reflection precipitated the worlds, and describes how the ten emanations or qualities of God are reflected downward to establish order in all departments of life. Additionally, the Zohar states that the principles do not descend to earth, but rather cast their shadows into the substance of matter.[4]

Moses Maimonides, author of *The Guide for the Perplexed*, states that the heart is in constant motion. It is the source of every motion one notices in the body, because it rules over all the other members, and through its own pulsation, communicates to them, the force required for their functions. The heart epitomizes the whole body. It consists of three parts—the inner, middle and outer part, which correspond to the cerebral, thoracic, and the abdominal cavities of the body. It also corresponds to the three main divisions of mind, spirit and body. According to *The Secret Work*, the heart is the only manifested God, because the two higher aspects— consciousness and intelligence— are definitely invisible and beyond the limitations of physical manifestation; the Spirit in the heart is the third and lowest aspect of the Supreme Essence. The third aspect of the Divine is the Lord of the Pulse, which is the only direct manifestation of Spirit in matter. This Pulse often referred to as the Heavenly Breath, is the rhythm of the Infinite. The pulse point is referred to as the drum of the Mother, the drum that beats the doom of every Man. More over the heart is not only the seat of so-called emotions, but also high Olympus, because it is said that the mountain of the gods rises above the four elements of fire, water, air, and earth until its peak is in ether, the fifth element. And in the utter tranquility of this fifth element, where the gods reside, is the place where is concealed a "small ether" and a spirit so vast that the universe can scarcely contain it.[5]

According to Ageless Wisdom, all bodies whether spiritual or material, have three bodies, whose center is spirit, and the circumference is matter. These three bodies are referred to as upper, middle and lower centers. The three universal centers represent three suns, or three aspects of the sun. These three centers have their analogue in the three grand centers of the human body—the head, the heart and the reproductive center. The first of these suns is analogous to the light inherent in the sun itself; the second corresponds to the light that immediately proceeds from the sun and the third, to the splendor communicated by this light to nature. Since the superior, or spiritual center, is in the midst of the other two, its analogue in the physical body is the heart, the most spiritual and mysterious organ in the human body.

All the mysteries recognize the heart as the center of spiritual consciousness. This concept is often ignored, and the heart is usually seen in the exoteric sense as a symbol of the emotional nature. But the heart is so central to the consciousness of the individual that it is important to recognize all its physical and non-physical aspects, as well as the fact that this is the place where the mental, emotional, and physical aspects of the individual come together to be expressed internally and externally. Any one who has attained the level of adeptship understands the human heart and knows what great struggles they face to maintain balance in the midst of the swirling conflicts of the world's emotional life. These souls are tender without being weak, compassionate without unduly identifying themselves with the woes of others, and they firmly correct error without feeling any condemnation for those who err.[6]

The heart is the Seat of Life and the Sun Center in the human body. The heart is central to the specific purpose for which Man was sent into incarnation, and so lets turn our attention to the Sun and the planetary influences, which impact that goal. The Sun has three aspects—the Physical Sun, which is oriented to multiplicity and the illusion of "manyness", separation, and the animal soul; the Heart of the Sun, oriented toward the human and the Divine soul, which has a true understanding of his essential duality; and finally, the Central Spiritual Sun which is associated with Divine Consciousness, the Will of the whole, Unity, and the awareness of God. Hermetic philosophers see the sun as the supreme benefactor of the material world, and believe that there is a Spiritual Sun which ministers to the human and universal needs of the invisible and the Divine part of Nature. With regard to this, Paracelsus writes:

> "There is an earthly sun, which is the cause of all heat, and all who are able to see, may see the sun; and those who are blind and cannot see him, may feel his heat. There is an Eternal Sun, which is the source of all wisdom, and those whose spiritual senses have awakened to life will see that sun, and be conscious of his existence; but those who have not attained spiritual consciousness may yet feel His Power by an inner faculty which is called Intuition."[7]

The planetary ruler of the heart, which is the Sun, is associated with the sign of Leo, and both are directly under the influence of the constellation of Sirius, which also wields the electric force for our planetary scheme. When humanity is perfected by the influences of Leo, he initially becomes a loving, self-conscious soul, who carries his power of expression straight through from his own plane to the plane of exterior manifestation, while maintaining internal control; later on, he becomes a true observer who is detached from the material side of life, but uses matter as he pleases.[8] *Sensitivity* sums up the whole story and function of the sign of Leo, since the objective of all astrological influences is the interaction of the self-conscious unit within the individual with its environment. The development of sensitive responses to the

123

impact of one's surroundings, and the ability stand at the center of one's little universe, as the Sun stands at the center, is an important influence of this sign. Man begins to realize that everything in his environment is contributing to his liberation, since the nature of all things is to set free rather than to bind, and he comes to know that the inherent tendency of self-existence is toward liberation, which is at the heart of the cosmic order. Ultimately, the spiritual sensitivity of the God-Man, which is the fusion of the soul and the personality, results in the Liberated Man who is no longer influenced by his environment, but now begins the arduous task of conditioning his life to the Divine plan and purpose, as well as to the sensitivity and impact of the higher worlds in fulfillment of the final goal, the liberation of humanity.

Everyone is here on this planet to achieve final initiation. And initiations are a process of penetration into the mysteries of the science of the Self, and of the one self in all selves; the Path of Initiation is the final stage on man's path of evolution, and it is divided into many stages. Initiation marks the transference of man's consciousness from his lower quaternary to his triad, resulting in fusion of his personality with his soul, or matter with spirit. Each individual is stimulated into awakening by an electric rod or scepter of power, which is designed to:

- Stimulate the latent fires until they blaze
- Synthesize the fires through an occult activity that brings them within a certain radius of each other
- Increase the vibratory activity of some centers, whether in ordinary man or the Heavenly Man
- Expand all bodies, especially the causal body

• Arouse the kundalini fire at the base of the spine and directs its upward movement systematically through the chakras[9]

The four scepters of power and initiation are— cosmic, systemic, planetary, and hierarchical. The scepter of power for our Solar sphere is in our Sun, and it is specifically hidden in the "Heart of the Sun", that mysterious and subjective sphere which lies behind our physical sun, and of which our physical sun is a shield or envelop.

The sign of Leo is where the consciousness of individuality is developed, used, and finally consecrated to its Divine purpose. Leo is also related to Polaris, the Pole Star in the Little Bear constellation, and is especially susceptible to the Pointer in the Great Bear. The Pole Star, esoterically speaking, is regarded as the *"star of re-orientation"*, which brings the individual back to his originating source by re-facing and recovering that which is lost. All adepts agree that in the main, what the aspirant has lost is his memory.

The energy from this Pointer is the influence, which guided man on his path of involution into matter. When the purpose for which man went into matter is achieved, the Pole Star begins to make its presence felt, and a sense of right direction, and guidance is registered in the cells of the aspirant, to re-orient him on his evolutionary path back to his source and to full consciousness. Leo rules the heart and the spine, and this influence gives the aspirant the "spine" and sense of "individuality" needed for him to symbolically stand on his own two feet. Leo is of paramount significance in the life of the aspirant, since he must know himself through true self-awareness before he can know that Divine Spirit is his true Self, and at the same time come to know his fellowman. It is here that the Divine Necessity of achieving alignment is portrayed in the symbolism of the sky and the sun as the source of Divine Intelligence. Once this alignment is achieved there is then an inflow of Divine energy, and man is linked in a new and creative way to the source of Divine Supply.[10]

Leo is the other half of the cosmic influence of the Age of Aquarius and must be remembered as a part of the great mystery of the Sphinx. The signs of Leo and Virgo make up the spirit and matter of the whole man, and the God-man. As a result, the true nature of the world and the Mystery of the Sphinx will be revealed at the same time. The mystery of the Sphinx is connected to the secret of the solar angels, to the mystery of the higher and lower mind, as well as to subjective and objective consciousness and their relationship to each other. The Sphinx is the propounder of the eternal riddle. In practical occultism, this riddle represents the supreme attainment which is the identification of the Inner Self of the personality with the Cosmic Self.[11] In this world cycle, the sign of the Sphinx is divided into two signs, Leo the Lion and Virgo the Virgin. This is so because the state of human evolution leads to the realization of recognized duality, until at "the judgment" a fusion takes place and Man's sense of antagonistic dualism begins to end.[12]

Individuality and self-consciousness are outstanding keynotes of the sign of Leo. It is important here to differentiate between self-consciousness motivated by instinct, and the desire of a truly developed Man. In the former instance, one recognizes himself as the dramatic center of his own universe, and is swayed by a desire and an orientation towards the satisfaction of that desire. In the latter case Man's direction, purpose and plan is oriented to that of the Divine Plan for humanity.[13] Another keynote of Leo is the will-to-illumine, which constitutes the driving urge towards self-knowledge, self-perception and intellectual positivity, the will-to-rule, and to dominate. This force conditions the aspirant on the path to move toward having dominion over nature as Adam was commanded to do in the Garden of Eden. The aspirant comes to learn that this statement is a direct reference to his gaining dominion over his own animal nature, which is facilitated by Leo, king of the jungle. He achieves self-mastery and control over his own personality, through this sign, since Leo represents the preparatory work that all individuals and all races must undertake in the process of their own return journey.

The three constellations, which control and energize our solar system, are: the Great Bear, Sirius, and the Pleiades, and the three great centers through which these constellations reflect their influence are: Shamballa, the Hierarchy, and Humanity. These three constellations work through the medium of the seven planetary rays and the twelve constellations, which form the great wheel of the zodiac. These three major energies are orchestrated by the Lords or ruling Powers, who mysteriously step down the forces of life through the seven sacred planets. This great inter-relation is embodied in the awesome process of Transmission, Reception, Absorption, Relation, and Living Activity— which embodies one of the most important clues to the whole evolutionary process, and is the key to the mystery of time and space, as well as the solution for all problems. The factor of greatest importance here is that the whole matter is a function of focused Will.[14]

The energies emanating from Sirius are linked to the love-wisdom aspect, or the attractive power of the Solar Logos to the Great Being. This great cosmic soul energy is related to the center of the Hierarchy, through which the Great White Lodge on Sirius finds outlet for its spiritual service in the Great White Lodge on Earth. The Sun is the heart of our planet and Sirius is the administrative Over Lord of our planet, our Sun, and the heart of the physical body. The center of our physical heart is called "the Heart of the Sun" and is also called the Holy of Holies, the location of the kingdom of heaven. Sirius, therefore, oversees the development and evolution of all consciousness on our planet. Consequently, it behooves us to take a closer look at this constellation and its objective as regard this experiment of which we are a part. As stated before, Sirius rules the sign of Leo, which rules August, the month of the Dog-star, called Sirius, which is the home of the greater Lodge to which the man on the path of initiation is admitted, and to which it brings him as a humble disciple. The Great White Lodge on Sirius is the spiritual prototype of the Great White Lodge on Earth of which modern Masonry is but a distorted reflection, just as the personality is a distorted reflection of the Soul.[15]

The three influences of Sirius are focused in the Regulus, usually referred to as "the Heart of the Lion", a white star of great magnitude in the constellation of Leo.[16]

The role of Venus, the energy of Love and Beauty, cannot be ignored in the affairs of the heart and the evolution of consciousness in man. All philosophers and sages conclude that she is the 'alter ego' of planet Earth, and therefore is primarily involved in the functioning of outcomes here. Her relationship with the Sun in Sirius focuses on the development of the lower and higher mental bodies of Man, and correspondingly, the quickening and strengthening of the heart. The force flows from the heart of the

Sun, working through the triangular relationship of Venus, the Sun, and the Earth.

It is important to note here that energies and forces are pouring into and upon our solar system and planet ceaselessly, potently, and cyclically. These energies come from all manner of sources extraneous to our solar and planetary scheme. However, until Man's bodily instruments become sensitive enough to register a definite response, scientists and astrologers alike will continue to deny their existence, but this does not in any way indicate that these energies and forces do not exist. It is partly for this reason that the Sun, through the energies of Leo, brings about these sensitivities in the heart and mind of mankind.

Venus rules the nerve plexus in Man's throat center, connecting the heart center to the head center, and linking the four lower centers in the body to two higher centers in the head. Alchemists say 'the sun rises to be joined to the moon", and the moon center is the pituitary body, or Master gland that controls all bodily functions; the sun center is the cardiac plexus in the upper trunk. Through the sun center in the body, contact can be made with the pure radiance of the Sun, and its metaphysical counterpart in the human body, and the body then receives what alchemical philosophers call *undifferentiated Prana*, which originates in the Sun. When the solar energy rises through the Venus center in the throat, the superconscious impulse received through the sun center is changed into the awakened functioning of the Venus center. The state of consciousness produced by the awakening of this throat center is predominantly emotional, because the desire nature is now stirred into intense activity. Venus is "the door", literally and symbolically, which has to initially open towards the heart rather than towards the head, at the beginning of the process of transformation. The secretions released into the bloodstream from the endocrine gland in the Venus center located in the throat begin to perform their subtler functions by awakening the individual to interior *hearing* and interior *sight*; and the aspirant actually begins to hear the Wise Men of the East. Later, this same door must swing the other way, to allow the force from the heart center to rise through the throat to enter and energize the brain. However, in order for any effective action to occur, there must be deep and genuine emotion, and the desire for peace must persist as the dominant motive. As a result, little or no progress can be made in the work of practical occultism by those who have only intellectual motives, since feelings which flow from the heart center, must be part of the process.[17]

All alchemists agree that behind the veil of language, the simple truth is this: "love is the fulfillment of the law. It is said that the pure gold of the Absolute is found through the working of the gentle heat of love, (and) that the sacrifice of sacrifices is a broken and contrite heart purified in the fires of love, and that only through love can the true pattern of that perfect golden cube, the New Jerusalem, be rightly perceived and understood"

The rose, which is also a symbol of Venus, is recognized as a symbol of secrecy. When the petals of the rose open up under the influence of the Sun, man will come to know his true relationship to his brother, and the Age of Brotherhood will then be our legacy.[18]

Gold is the metal assigned by alchemists to the Sun, and the gold of religious thought is absolute and supreme reason. In philosophy, it is truth. In the subterraneous and mineral world, it is the purest and most perfect gold. In visible nature, it is the Sun, which is the emblem of the "Sun of Truth", as the Sun is the shadow of the First Source from which all splendors spring. For this reason, it is said the search for the Magnum Opus is called the search for the Absolute, and the Great Work is itself called "The Work of the Sun."[19]

Chapter Seven

THE SHEKINAH, THE MYSTERY OF SEX

"The Indivisible Point, which has no limit and cannot be comprehended because of its purity and brightness, expanded from without, forming a brightness, and served the indivisible Point as a veil;" yet the latter also could not be veiled in consequence of its immeasurable light. It too expanded from without, and this expansion was its garment. Thus, through a constant upheaving motion, finally, the world originated. The Spiritual substance sent forth by the Infinite Light is the first Sephira, Shekinah, which contains all the other nine Sephiroth within her. Esoterically, she contains but two, the active masculine potency whose Divine name is Jah, and the passive potency, Intelligence, represented by the Divine name Jehovah.(Zohar)

The Secret Doctrine, Volume 11, H. P. Blavatsky, page355

CHAPTER SEVEN

The Shekinah, the Mystery of Sex

No examination of the Feminine Principle can be complete without deciphering the mystery of Shekinah, who, Ageless Wisdom says, is one and the same with the Mystery of Sex. In this chapter, I will re-state in the simplest form possible, the powerful treatise put forward by Arthur. E. Waite in his book *Holy Kabbalah: the Higher Secret Doctrine*, which is an interpretation of the Zohar, while maintaining the accuracy and integrity of Waite's work.

Let us not forget that She is the Divine Presence that walked in the Garden of Eden in the cool of the evening, who went before Israel in the desert as a pillar of cloud by day, and as a pillar of fire by night, as they fled from bondage in Egypt. Just as mankind is now fleeing the symbolic "Egypt", the land of bondage, we are assured that Shekinah, the Holy Ghost, who is none other than the Divine Mother we were promised at the end of the Piscean Age, will again lead humanity into the Promised Land.

The Kabbalah, known as "the Reception", is said to be the cup out of which the mystery of the Shekinah, issues. It states that the sole objective for which the One Life sent mankind into the world of matter is for him to know that God the Father and God the Mother are one and the same. Once this conscious knowing is achieved, the heart experiences true bliss. The Shekinah is the mystery of Man and God, of man who was made in the likeness of God, and the relationship between all things, which are above, with all things, which are below. The synthesis of the Written and Oral Laws is the Mystery of Faith in which entails the intercourse and celestial union of the spirit for work upon the Earth.

Shekinah is known by the following names in the four worlds:

- Eheyeh, in the world of Fire
- Yod-Heh-Vav-Heh, in the world of Water
- Elohim, in the world of Air
- Adonai, in the Earth

She is called by every name, and is of every designation. In the Earth and Above the Earth *all* ascriptions, without exception, are feminine. She is at one time the Daughter of the King; at another, she is the Betrothed, the Bride, the Mother, and at the same time, she is the sister in relation to the world of Man at large. There is also a sense in which this Daughter of God is, and at the same time becomes, the Mother of Man, but in respect to the manifest universe, she is the architect of worlds, acting in response to the Word uttered by God in creation.[1]

In what Ageless Wisdom calls the myth of Paradise, Shekinah is considered to be Eden itself. Above, She is the place from which the river of life flows, and below She is, in fact, the Waters of the Garden. This too is Shekinah, because She is conceived externally as Bride, Daughter, and Sister in the world below. In respect to Divine Womanhood in the transcendent world, she is Matrona, the one who unites with the King for the perfection of the Jehovah, the Divine Male, who is at the same time, Elohim, the Divine Female. Elohim, the Divine Feminine, is herself a trinity in respect to her title of Elohim. There is an Elohim in transcendence who is concealed and mysterious; an Elohim that judges above, and an Elohim who judges below, but these three are in fact one. The Oral Law is her image, while the image of Jehovah is the Written Law, about which there are significant distinctions, because the Inward Law is Life itself, while the Outer Law is the body of life. She is the waters that are above the firmament in respect to her title as Elohim, and she is also the waters below the firmament, when she manifests as Adonai. As Elohim, she is the Middle Pillar on the Tree of Life, and all aspects of the One Thing. She abides in all, and at the same time, she is above and below, within and without. The Zohar wants to show here in the most positive and unqualified way that the Shekinah is female in the essential aspect, whether it relates to her being the Bride of God, in the transcendent state where there is no distinction between her and the Holy One, or in her role as the guide to humanity. In all her characteristics and her missions, she is always typically female, comprising all women in the mystery of who she is.[2]

In the Book of Eziekiel 23: 20, the Shekinah is described as the Liberating Angel— manifesting as both male and female, who delivers the world in all ages. When Shekinah dispenses the celestial benediction to the world below, she expresses as male, but when charged with offices of judgment, she expresses as female. To understand these male and female attributes is what the Path of Initiation is about, and in this process of knowing, the interchange of sex in Divine things must come to be thoroughly understood.[3] Metatron, the supreme blessedness of the Soul in heaven, is an aspect of Shekinah, who is indifferently male or female, depending on the vibration it is in union with. Shekinah is to Metatron what the Sabbath is to the weekdays, meaning that she is rest, also the rapture of rest, and at the same time, it is that rest in which the intercourse of union occurs. While the Zohar does not claim authority, it states that on the issue of sex as it relates to Shekinah, the Divine Name Adonai answers to the male aspect, Shekinah to the female, and Elohim to the combination of both.

As regards the Shekinah's relation to the Tree of Life, or what is called the Sepirothic Tree—with its many attributions and references—the one that is most dominant is the Middle Pillar of Benignity, which extends from the top of the Tree, Kether, to the bottom of the Tree, Malkuth. In this Middle Pillar, she takes on all the emanations or Sephiroth, to God or the Crown, and even beyond height and depth, to the plane of undifferentiated reality— Ain Soph. The Middle Pillar has been described as the trunk of the tree, and it is the journey through Shekinah, and her glorious leading that takes Man on his return journey back to the Crown. But of course, She is at the same time also the embodiment and synthesis of all the emanations of the Tree.

The fifty gates of understanding are assigned to the sphere of Binah on the Tree of Life, symbolizing the return of Man to the heights of spiritual union through the influence of Shekinah. These fifty gates of understanding are related to the human body's seven chakras, which we call the seven planetary forces. The seven chakras are reputed to have seven sub-levels, with a total of forty-nine gateways, or doorways, to enlightenment— plus one, Binah, the Gate through which mankind returns from his journey into matter. Man attains this in and because of Shekinah; and for this reason her number is said to be fifty, even though she is not contained within that number.

The complete integration of all the branches of the Tree of Life will not occur until Adam, the Son of Man, who we call Shiloh, comes. For it is He who is the Redeemer of the Redeemed of Earth. The Shekinah is in Chokmah the sphere of wisdom, and this relationship is both concealed and visible, thereby reconciling the mysteries above with the mysteries below. Her hidden nature refers to the Supreme Degree of the Divine Essence of which She is, and which is beyond understanding. She is revealed in wisdom by the Law of Mercy. On one side of the Tree She is Mercy, while at the same time, on the other side of the Tree, severity proceeds from her.[4]

When she expresses from the side of the Father, she is Chokmah, but from the side of the Mother, she is Binah. In truth, she is on both sides of the Tree, and is the Spirit of all the Holy Assemblies above, and below. We should also remember that in the physical order, it is woman who conceives, contains, and brings forth both male and female.

The apparent attributions to Shekinah as feminine in her threefold aspect provide us with a key—she is the catholic nature of womanhood in all degrees and grades. In connection with her work in creation, as architect of the world, the Word was uttered to her, was conceived by her, and was brought or begotten into execution through her; Shekinah below concurred with the Architect above, who was also a builder, but her work in the creation of the perfect temple below remains unfinished. On the manifest side, the history of Shekinah herself begins in the Garden of Eden, and according to another symbol, she is the Garden itself, the counterbalance to this being that Shekinah was the companion of humans in exile when Adam and Eve were expelled from the Garden, as evidenced in the story of Israel, or humanity's exile into matter. It was Shekinah who walked with Adam in Paradise under the title of Lord God.[5] As we know, transgression followed and our prototypical parent was driven out of the Garden. This act might appear to mean that man was driven out from under the wings of Shekinah, but in fact he was not deserted in his need, because she followed him into the captivity of his five senses; and according to the Zohar, Shekinah suffered with mankind, or, as it was more accurately put: "Man was driven out, and the Mother was driven out with him." While this was the primal captivity, the Mother shared in all the captivities that followed. It is said that she is the sacrifice, which God placed on His right hand and on His left hand, and round about Him. However, this separation between the King and Matrona in the outer world brought about a separation in the Divine Name; and although it is forbidden, even in thought, to separate the Heavenly Bride and Bridegroom, this has come about through the sufferings of Israel, with whom Shekinah was destined to endure from the beginning. Accordingly, when Israel, who is humanity, is in exile, Shekinah is also in exile. The Holy One will remember his covenant with humanity, or Israel, because his covenant is with Shekinah. The meaning of this act is that she is with the elect, for better or for worse, for richer or for poorer, in their attainments, and in their sins, though not in the same manner. Her shame is the defiled body of humanity; and she is said to be in separation from the King because of the wickedness of Man; and though she does not leave man, the sin of humanity causes her to turn away.[6]

In summary, she was driven out of the Garden of Eden like a wife sent away by her husband, but it was for the salvation of world. There is a Shekinah called servant, and a Shekinah called the Daughter of the King, the one who is above the angels, as described in the Christian doctrine, and is called *Regina Angelorum*. In respect to the rest of creation, she is like the soul is to the body; and she is the body to the Holy One, though She and God are one. She is the Mistress of the Celestial School called the Abode of the Shepherds, which is the school of Metatron, and is recognized as a form assumed by Shekinah. She was present when Isaac blessed Jacob, and it was She who conferred upon Jacob the name of Israel, and who was with him when he set up the mystic stone as a pillar. In her aspect of Male and Father, she presided over the birth, the sustainance and the liberation of the twelve tribes of Israel, bringing Moses into form for the purpose of freeing the children from bondage in Egypt, and She then accompanied them in their wanderings through the desert. She it was who led them as the cloud by day and the fire by night. She led Moses through the clouds to Mount Sinai, where he was given the law book, and he caused Shekinah to manifest in the Ark of the Covenant over the Mercy seat between the two Cherubims in the Holy of Holies in Solomon's Temple, Her residenc on Earth. Simultaneously, she occupies a corresponding residence erected above in Heaven, where her counterpart Metatron resides. While many scholars debate whether Shekinah is the same as the Holy Spirit, they conclude that spirit can be distinguished in three ways as:

• The Spirit below, which is called the Holy Spirit
• The Spirit of the Middle Way, which is that of Wisdom and Understanding

- The Spirit which sounds the trumpet and unites the fire to water— this is the Superior, Concealed and Mysterious Spirit.[7]

Traditional belief is that at the hour when Moses, the true prophet, was to be born, the Holy One caused the Holy Spirit to come forth as Skekinah from the Tabernacle, the abode of its transcendence. And, it was Shekinah who overshadowed him with Divine splendor, entrusting him with the keys of power that would enlighten a thousand worlds. Those who witnessed this knew that the Holy One had resolved to change the face of the world through his servant Moses, whose glory was so bright that when he descended from the mountain of illumination homage was paid to him, because this state of power and light he now possessed enabled him to smite Pharaoh and his whole country.

One of the most important considerations to come out of this whole subject is the Cohabiting or Indwelling Glory, referred to as Shekinah in both the Holy Scripture and the Zohar. We know that this Presence dwelt between the Cherubims in the Tabernacle, or Ark of Moses. The Cherubims are said to have been male and female, and are in reality types in the Sanctuary of Israel, and their manifestation on Earth, is of a type, in turn, of the union that is above. When a *mean* of all references is taken, the conclusion will be that Shekinah is the principle of Divine Motherhood. She is the feminine side of Divinity, and the office of the mother on earth is made sacred by its archetype in heaven.

The primary reason for decoding the Secret Doctrine is to gain insight into which aspect of the Divine Nature or Principle is realizable by the heart of Man. It is meaningless to decode these bodies of ancient knowledge unless they have something definite to tell us concerning the way, the truth, and the life of which

Man's relationship and obligation to his brother is central. In this respect, it is therefore reassuring to know that whosoever wrongs a poor person is guilty of wronging Shekinah, because she is the protectress of the poor.[8]

The Mystery of Sex, which is undoubtedly the Mystery of Shekinah, concerns the whole subject of the Indwelling Glory. This Mystery is everywhere present, but the concealed and coded wording suggests that the entrance of the High Priest into the Holy of Holies belongs to the Mystery of Sex. It is said that Shekinah dwelt with Israel prior to the captivity (probably the captivity in Babylon) and that the sin, which brought about this exile, was equivalent to the uncovering of the hidden, physical center of Shekinah. This unveiling refers to the Minerva or Diana of Israel, whose veil like that of Isis is never lifted by Man.[9] As recorded in the history of Man it was through the intermediation of Woman that the Mystery of Shekinah, which comprises all women, abides with him who is united to woman. In one of her aspects, she is the *type* of stainless womanhood, but she always passes into espousal below, as she is ever in espousal above, for the fulfillment of herself in humanity, and of all humanity in her.[10] The glorious canticle of the Song of Solomon reveal the history of the beginning and the end of all that belongs to the union of the Mystery of the Lover and the Beloved, throughout the ages. The summary of the Holy Scriptures, the work of creation, the mystery of the patriarchs, the exile in Egypt, the exodus of Israel, the Decalogue, and the manifestation on Sinai, symbolize all the events that occurred during the sojourn in the desert, during the entrance into the Holy Land of Caanan, and in the building of the Holy Temple. It also summarizes the dispersal of Israel throughout all the nations, and its deliverance to come as well as the resurrection of the dead, and the events leading up to the Sabbath, the day of rest.

Like a tree, Man, was uprooted and planted anew on the plane of matter to disperse and complete the Sacred Name in all directions of the Earth. He was commanded to increase and multiply, to procreate and produce children, and to spread the radiance of the Sacred Name in every direction, by collecting spirits and souls, which would constitute the glory of the Holy One above and below. Importantly, it is through this process of procreation, through the union of male and female that the descent of the Divine glory can be made manifest on earth. The clear implication here is that the Holy One accomplishes unions in the world above, before the descent of souls to earth, which explains why the union of man and woman below is modeled on or reflective of the union of the Divine Masculine and Divine Feminine above. In fact, the Divine is said to intervene and overshadow man and woman in marriage, with the primary intent of populating the planet, so that God above could dwell below. Hence, it is important that man and woman be tempered in spirit, that the heart and mind of the Lover and the Beloved be raised from the physical to a spiritual degree, i.e. from the Mode of Nature into the Mode of Grace, and to the Most Holy Shekinah, which indwells and cohabits during the external act. During the act, the Divine secret essence enters the body of the woman and is joined with the divine essence of the man physically and spiritually, so that both spirits are melded together and the spiritual interchange between bodies is constantly taking place. The indistinguishable state that arises creates a situation where it can almost be said that the male is with the female, and is neither male nor female; in truth they are both and neither, and as such,

Man is affirmed to be composed of the world above, which is male, and of the female world below; the same is true of woman. The Songs of Solomon further indicate in their provocative language of joy and desire, and simultaneously in an alternate language, that all things are formed above according to a pattern which is faithfully reproduced below, and so it is held and follows that once desire awakens beneath, it also awakens on high.[11]

It is vital to note here that there are two classes of espousals in which the need for exaltation occurs, and their duties differ in relation to the fulfillment of the Divine demand. There are ordinary mortals whose conjugal relations are sanctified in a plenary sense, and then there are the Sons of the Doctrine, those selected from among the chosen thousands, for the purpose of studying the Law. These Sons of the Doctrine reserve conjugal relations and praise for the Sacred Name of God for the night of the Sabbath— the moment when the Holy One is united to the Community of Israel above.[12] An essential principle is that Man must be attached to his wife in order for the Shekinah to ever be with him. He could study the Secret Doctrine by night and by day, but this cannot lead to a true life, in spite of the practiced holiness of the intellectual. The plain truth is that Man must not be alone, as was indicated by the finding of a helpmate for Adam in the Garden of Eden. The many Sons of Israel and students of the Doctrine in the Middle Ages who traveled in search of wisdom, were also men of affairs and workers in the vineyard of the world, as well as in the Garden of God, but before going on these journeys, they were required to secure the protection and consolation of Shekinah, receiving instructions from Her as they moved forward on their journey. They did this because it was important for them not to separate themselves from the Shekinah, and in addition they asked the

Holy One to watch over all their actions during their absence from home to ensure that they would not be separated from their spiritual companion. Thus the Cohabiting Glory accompanied the Sons of the Doctrine on their travels and ventures, becoming their overshadowing grace and power. They were then always aware of a certain marriage in their relationship with her, of becoming, spiritually, a spouse of the soul. On their return, they were obligated to give nuptial gratification to the wives, heart to heart, and face to face, seeing that they had had the advantage of mystical union with their Helpmate or Companion who is on high, during their absence. The work of the Sons of the Doctrine, both at home and abroad, is essential to the work of Shekinah above and below, within the household and without, ensuring that peace and harmony are maintained on all planes. Indeed, the Supreme Mystery, the Mystery of Sex, cannot be revealed to a Man who is unmarried. It is said that as long Jacob remained unmarried, God did not manifest clearly to him, because only in a committed relationship that the distinction between the perfection above, and the perfection below, becomes complete in Man, and God is able to manifest to him clearly. When, at the moment of his conjugal relations, Man has the Shekinah in his view, and the pleasure he experiences is a meritorious work, in this conjugal union, if there are any offspring, the Heavenly companion provides a holy soul for the newborn child. The union below is an image of the union above. And this is the mystery of the Mother in transcendence, who abides with the male only in as far as he has constituted himself a house by his attachment to a female, since there must be a local habitation—i.e. a union below— to offer a point of contact with the union that is on high. And so, the Divine Mother pours her blessings down on the male and the female in equal measure.

The male below is then said to be encompassed by two females, as all the blessings of the two worlds are opened before him, and in this way, Shekinah also creates the image of herself below. The Holy experience with Shekinah, and the physical experience with his wife, who symbolizes Shekinah below, enables him to read the Secret Doctrine of womanhood on earth. It is read to him by she who sits between the Pillars of the Eternal Temple with the Book of the Secret Law lying open on her sacred lap— She is none other than the High Priestess, the Female Elder of the Temple. The Book of the Law that she holds, reveals the correct relationship of the spirits on the two sides of the Tree of Life; and Man receives proof that the spirits of the evil side respect the superiority of those on the side of goodness (Mankind) who, being provided with bodies, can fulfill the duties of procreation.

The object of the union of the Matron with the Heavenly King is to send down holy souls into this world, and in turn, their colleagues on earth seek to attract these sacred souls into their own children. Simply put, the theory of conception is that the Holy One and his Shekinah provide the soul, while the father and the mother between them provide the body, and then heaven and earth, the stars of heaven as well as the angels are associated with the formation. At the moment of intercourse, the Man's desire for the woman and her for him, is mutual and balanced once *their seeds are* interblended to produce a child. There are two aspects to this:— firstly, the child born of this Divine union will be superior to that of other men. Secondly, since its birth resulted from the desire of the Tree of Life, it therefore draws life from its father and its mother. Hence we are obligated to receive sanctification for all souls brought into manifestation and incarnate life. This explains why the Sons of the Doctrine, who know the Mysteries of the Doctrine, turned all their thoughts to God, and their children were called Sons of the King. Children born of marital relations that are frigid, uninspiring, purely legal and contrived, are not encompassed with this sanctity, and caused a breach in the world above.[13]

The Mystery of Faith forms the basis of earthly espousals and marriages. The words *"male and female created he them"* are indicative of an intelligence that is inaccessible to humans, and as an object of faith, this expresses the Supreme Mystery that constitutes the glory of God, the mystery by which Man, heaven, and earth were created. The Adam Kadmon is seeded in this Mystery, which is why it is said that God blessed the male and the female and called them Adam when they were created. This Mystery also contains the examination of good and evil, which it then integrates. Zion represents severity, and Jerusalem, mercy, but the two are one, just as the black pillar and the white pillar are one. On the Tree of Life, goodness and mercy are on the male side, while evil and severity are on the female side, but these two must be united by the Middle Pillar, under the wings of Shekinah, who is the Middle Pillar itself; and once this is accomplished, joy, beauty and goodness are found everywhere.[14]

The human body is said to contain forty-nine gates of compassion called chakras, which relate to the seven planetary forces and their seven sub-levels. These chakras are connected with the mystery of the perfect Man, who is composed of male and female, and the Mystery of Faith. They are the Gates of Understanding that refer to Binah, the Sphere of the Mother on the Tree of Life, and to Shekinah the Spouse in Transcendence who also dwells there. However, according to legend, there is a fiftieth gate, which Moses did not open. This is the Gate of the Mystery of Espousals in the Divine World, which emanates from the side of Severity on the Tree of Life, but is unknown to humanity, who is Israel, because he is in exile. Nevertheless, the Man who devotes himself to the study of the Law Book, held by the woman between the two pillars, opens the Fiftieth Gate. Moses attained the level represented by these Gates, and without this attainment, Spiritual Israel would still be in bondage in Egypt. Finally, this Fiftieth Gate, which is the synthesis of all Gates, in conjunction with the One Degree, which is the synthesis of all Degrees, allows us entrance into the glory of the Holy One. A conscious knowledge of these seven forces in the body, which are equivalent to the Seven Degrees, and the Seven Palaces, reveals the Mysteries of Faith.

After what is symbolically termed the end of the world, a kingdom will come with the advent of the Messiah, which will indicate perfect conformity in the nuptial state, above as well as below. Some of the many citations connected with this Mystery are:

- The union of male and female
- A spring which flows forever
- A well fed by a spring— a fountain of gardens
- A fountain sealed— the well of living waters and streams from Lebanon
- The Moon— another symbol of Shekinah

Complete understanding of the Mystery of Faith is to *know* that Jehovah is Elohim, and that the creation of man in the image of Elohim is an allusion to the Mystery of the Male and Female Principles. When Divine Fire and the Divine Water are united, they give birth to that river which *"went forth from Eden to water the Garden"*, the River of Life and the River of Souls. The Higher

Eden, the place of Divine Nuptials and the Garden, which is watered by the river, is the place of nuptials below. We now understand in what sense Shekinah is called the Supreme Mother, and why through the bliss of heart one knows that Jehovah is Elohim, that Gentile is Jew, Black is White, Above is Below, Within is Without, and that the attainment of such knowledge is the purpose for which the Holy One sent Man into this world. This is the Mystery of Faith, which is the synthesis of the whole Law, and this Mystery— the source of all other Mysteries, is rooted in the Mystery of Experience in Man. When Israel or Humanity becomes perfected, man will make no distinction between any of the pairs of opposites. The descent of Shekinah, on the central path from Kether to Malkuth, testifies to the fact that she was destined from the beginning to suffer with humanity, and that the nuptial intercourse, which was infinitely holy and pure in the world above, descended through what is termed the *Fall* of Man into the region of the order of animal things. The alliance that Jehovah has with Elohim corresponds to the Covenant between God and Man, and only through the path of purification by water and fire can the soul of Man either penetrate the vestibule of Paradise, or else be repulsed from the world above.

We must understand that the union of humanity below is a reflection of the Divine Union. And the union between God and the Soul is, in a sense, often a vision, and indicative of a deeper stage. That Blessed Vision is the sight of the Shekinah and the contemplation of her Divine Face. She, who is the way, which leads to the Tree of Life, is herself the Tree, is kept by the Cherubim and the Flaming Sword, and is the Grand Matrona herself. She is the way of the Sacred City, the way of the Heavenly Jerusalem, the intermediary of communication between things above and below in both directions and the perfect Mediatrix— the repository of all the Divine Powers. She entrusted these Divine Powers to Enoch when he became Metatron, (also known as the *"young man"),* and charged him with the government of Earth.[15]

As the Sons of Doctrine, trod the forty-nine steps to perfect union through the fiftieth gate, they come to realize that all depends on thought, and that man is defiled by his thoughts. He, who at the moment of fulfilling the act of intercourse with his wife in the physical world, thinks of another woman, not only changes the Degree above, but also the Degree of Holiness into an impure one. In the same way, when humanity thinks of separation instead of Unity, and denies that Jehovah is Elohim, he causes impurity in his heart. However, there are two important facts to remember here: one that there is no lawful act of life, nor is there any Law of Nature which cannot be raised above its own degree by the consecration of motive, and two, that the will of man in all its authorized ways can be united to Divine Will. In other words, the students of the Secret Doctrine found that there is a Mystery of Nuptials, which ordinary man has not yet conceived of in his heart under the common motives of desire. Those to whom this mystery is revealed have already attained and fulfilled the Law with respect to marriage, and seek no new way of the physical kind; they were not lovers of the "white heat" and on a quest to find the ideal beloved; they were not in search of an excuse to set aside the old pledges and the old bonds; they sought to make all things in their life holy through the sanctity of their intentions for fulfilling the Law of Life, which directed them to increase and multiply. The Students discover and then conclude that the mystical marriages of the Eastern philosophy, of the Catholic Church, of the Mystical Jew, and of Latin Orthodoxy, have, over two thousand years, shared a similar understanding of the Sacramental Rites of marriage, and that the goal of these marriages, and of mystical intercourse is to beget children from what is called the *Holy Side* that is, Children of Grace rather than Children of Nature, although Grace is really only Nature better understood.[16]

The Sons of the Doctrine were not ascetics, nor solitaries, but a company of scholars in the city, the countryside, in villages and in the wilderness. In essence they were students of life, who came to realize the Divine Presence in their own hearts as a consequence of their own consecrated lives. They came to realize the world of Nature was Grace externalized, that the Divine Presence was everywhere, and that each one attained to that Union with the Presence in his own way by what is appropriate for his own heart and mind. They realized that there is NOTHING that is not Shekinah. They discovered the true meaning of the words *"It is not good for man to be alone"*, and that there is a very secret path in which "the joy of living honorably with his wife may bring the completed man, male and female, into the spiritual city of joy, (and into) the great city of praise, wherein is the joy of the Lord."[17]

Qabalah assigns the thirty-first path on the Tree of Life to Shin, which is Shekinah, the Life Breath of Creative Powers and Perpetual Intelligence. She is the electric fire, which is the source of all activities in both the macrocosm and the microcosm. The activities of this path are said to subside at the end of a particular cosmic cycle, and although it moves from its active to its latent state, it does not cease to be, because it is perpetual, eternal, and without beginning or end. For this reason Shekinah is known as Perpetual Intelligence.[18]

Chapter Eight

THE UNVEILED AND REVEALED ISIS-
THE GATE AND THE KEY

"When the Son separates from the Mother, he becomes the Father,"
the diameter standing for Nature, or the Feminine Principle.
Therefore, it is said: "In the world of being, the one point fructifies the
Line—The Virgin Matrix of Kosmos (the egg-shaped zero)— and
the immaculate Mother gives birth to the form that combines all forms."
The Secret Doctrine, Volume 1, H.P. Blavatsky, page 91

The Unveiled and Revealed Isis

The sign of Virgo, which the Virgin Mother symbolizes, is considered one of the most significant in the zodiac because it is concerned with the whole evolutionary process for which the Mother brought consciousness into matter. Her purpose is to shield, nurture and finally reveal the spiritual reality which every form hides or veils. The human form, however, is the most fitted and equipped to manifest spirit in a way that is different to any other expression of divinity and it is also best able to make objective and tangible the Divine Idea for which the whole creative process was intended.[1]

In the allegoric story of the Amazons, Hercules, the Sun-God, overcomes the nine-headed Hydra or serpent of desire, by being forced to his knees, and from that position of humility gains deliverance by lifting the serpent in the air. This story alludes to the lifting up of the Hydra of passion, hate, greed, ambition, selfishness, and aggression into the region of the soul; by so doing, Hercules was wrested out of the hands and grasp of the goddess of form, signifying the emergence of spiritual man from the control of matter. The three goddesses Eve, Isis and Mary, are of peculiar and significant importance in all world religions of our civilization because they embody the symbology of the entire form of nature. When integrated and functioning, these three aspects of the Mother of Form, represent the personality vehicle, which consists of the mental, emotional and physical bodies. The personality vehicle is symbolic of Humanity itself, and is an expression of the third aspect of Divinity— that of God the Holy Spirit, the Active, Intelligent, Nurturing Principle of the universe. Virgo, becomes the Mother of the Christ Child, who nurtures the unfoldment of a self-conscious entity who emerges when the personality vehicle is perfected.

Eve represents the mental nature and the mind of Man, who is attracted by the lure of knowledge to be gained through the experience of incarnation. Some say that Eve represents the emotional aspect of the Mother, but others agree that she represents the mind and the conscious decision to take humanity on the journey into matter; to this end, she took the apple of knowledge from the serpent of matter, and started the long human undertaking of experiment, experience, and expression, initiated in the Aryan cycle, designed to progress humanity along the path of evolution from the mental angle.

Creation stories in almost every religion speak of the separation of the Jehovah Elohim into two separate entities. Clarification of this believed separation is crucial and it is to this that we now turn our attention. In Christianity, those two beings are called Adam and Eve, and we are told that Eve was created, by taking a rib from the side of Adam. Ageless Wisdom, however, sees this understanding as very simplistic reasoning, and offers a different explanation instead. A dominant esoteric school of thought explains the creation of the sexes and how Adam and Eve became two instead of the androgynous existence they are said to embody, quite differently. It claims that the division resulted from a suppression of one pole of the androgynous being in order that the vital energies manifesting through that pole might be diverted toward the development of rational faculties in the material world. From this perspective, Man is still androgynous and spiritually complete, but in the material world, the feminine part of Man's nature, and the masculine part of woman's nature are in repose. The thinking is that knowledge of the Mysteries is imparted to Man as he goes through the process of spiritual unfoldment by the revelation of his soul. In this process, the latent element in each nature is gradually brought into activity, and the human being gradually regains his sexual equilibrium, with the woman being elevated from the position of Man's wandering half, to one of complete equality. Marriage is then regarded as companionship in which two complete individualities manifesting opposite polarities are brought into association with each other, resulting in an awakening of the latent qualities in each other and thus precipitating the attainment of each other's completeness. In essence, marriage is therefore just a means to the end. The end being the acknowledgement of the infinite potentialities of Divine completeness in both aspects of creation.[2]

One of the most destructive and malicious theological dogmas states, that Mankind has allegedly been cursed because of Adam and Eve's disobedience in the Garden of Eden. This fallacious teaching needs to be disposed of entirely since it must be borne in mind that Man's creative powers are a gift of Divine wisdom, not the result of sin. This argument is reinforced by the apparently paradoxical behavior of Jehovah who, at one moment, curses Adam and Eve, or Humanity, and at the next moment blesses them as his chosen people by telling them to "be fruitful and multiply (and) replenish the Earth." Ageless Wisdom suggests that this occurrence took place at the end of the sinless Third Root Race, under the law of a great periodical and geological period, and the beginning of the Fourth Root Race, which was characterized by the infant stages of the development of the mental instrument and the intellect. The Secret Doctrine teaches that for the spiritual primeval intelligence to achieve full Divine God consciousness, he must pass through the human stage, which means he must pass beyond the merely terrestrial human stage to achieve equilibrium between spirit and matter. Man must win the right to become Divine through self-experience; he must become a Thinker, and he must attain clear self-consciousness, which means he must become "Man." With the advent of mind, and the evolution of the Fourth Root Race—the Atlantean Race, Man began to think himself into separation, and enmity between brothers emerged. This is what is called the Serpent's seed, or the product of *Karma* and Divine Wisdom. The seed of the woman, or Lust, *bruised the head* of the seed of the *fruit of wisdom and knowledge*, by turning the holy mystery of procreation into animal gratification, an act that gradually changed the nature of the Fourth Root Race physiologically, morally, physically and mentally.[3]

The end of the Fourth Root Race was characterized by a wide gap, which had developed between the sons of materialism, and the energy of light, precipitated by a war between the Lords of Form and the Lords of Being from the Great White Lodge on Sirius, and other beings extraneous to our planetary life. After long periods of disaster and chaos, this battle resulted in victory for the Lords of Light, and brought an abrupt end to the Atlantean

Civilization, culminating in the catastrophic destruction of large numbers of human beings.[4] The nucleus, which was saved formed the basis of our present root race, the Aryan Race, also referred to as the Fifth Root Race or the Fifth Life Wave, which is scattered among every race on earth. It is important to note that this nucleus was formed from remnants of the Atleantean Race, the Indo-Germanic people, and some say, the Jewish race also, who were the first to help root the new developments of this Fifth Life Wave into the consciousness of humanity as a whole. The great body of arcane knowledge left to humanity by the Masters of Wisdom is specifically directed to this Fifth Life Wave, of which all humanity are members, and concerns the problems and opportunities it faces.[5] A close look at the Germanic people helps us understand what the Divine Mother, through her surrogate Eve, is working out through Man on the mental plane and in this Fifth Life Wave. We also need to keep in mind that the problems and opportunities with which we are faced began in Atlantean times, and must now be fought out to the finish. The conflicts we face as a human race have their root not only in human weakness and selfishness, but also in the situation that has existed for Ages between the Lodge of Masters of the Great White Lodge and the Lodge of Black Adepts, and the times we are now living in bear witness to the battle being played out between these two groups. The psychology of the Germanic peoples is typified by an age-old tendency to dominate, to take what is not their own, to regard themselves as unique and superior, and to view themselves as the embodiment of a super-race. There is a fixed and selfish determination on behalf of their own interests to plunge other nations and races into war, as reflected in the two world wars of the 20th century.[6] Many of these tendencies can also be observed in the Jewish peoples, who insist they are a chosen people, and by extension, these tendencies can be observed in humanity as a whole. So, let me hasten here to remind us all that we are ALL members of this Fifth Life Wave, and we ALL signed up for this experiment and experience. Which is why, I have great compassion for all groups of people who have volunteered to play out their particular role on this life stage. The Masters of Wisdom, also called the Lords of Compassion, have no judgment of humanity. Instead, they have great compassion because they know the journey every Man must walk in order to remember his relationship to his brother, who is his reflector. They work to help humanity achieve conscious love—a love defined as a process of determining action on the basis of the ultimate good of the individual or the group, where the immediate reactions of the personality are secondary. In this regard, those who oversee the evolution of humanity's consciousness are concerned with the final issue—the future welfare and ultimate well-being of humanity, and less concerned with the immediate suffering and pain of the personalities involved. Therefore, in every culture and every religion there is now a sense of expectancy for a turning point in the present reality, because we intuitively know that when the fullness of time has come, the Mother will bring forth the Child with which she has been pregnant—a liberated humanity.

Let us now look at the importance and dual role of Egypt in our collective past and in our future destiny. The Egyptian art of alchemy, known as the Hermetic Qabalah, has been long known to Europe as being related to the Judiac Qaballah, with Egypt being recognized as its place of origin. The Land of Egypt, into which the children of Israel were taken during captivity, is what Qabalists assign to the part of the body below the region of the kidneys. And it is out of Egypt that Moses, the illumined mind, as his name implies, led the twelve tribes or faculties of Israel, by raising the brazen serpent in the wilderness. This raising refers to the serpent power of the Kundalini, which is located at the base of the spine in the Saturn center.

The following allegorical story is about the journey of this Fifth Life Wave, the central character being the son of German Nobility. The story is the journey of this German lad on the path of Initiation, and this is the journey that everyone is making symbolically, literally, and unconsciously towards Jerusalem, the city of peace. The story is told by a distinguished Brother of the Invisible Order of Masters, who identifies himself in the manifesto called the *Fama Fraternitatis,* which was first circulated among German occultists in 1610 as Brother C.R.C.[7] This Brother, though an adult man, is described in this allegory as a *five* years old lad. He knows that to be a member of this True and Invisible Rosicrucian Order of Initiates, one must *become* a member; one cannot *join* this Order. He therefore sets out on the journey to become, and to know. The first stage of his journey to the Holy Land involves being placed in a cloister, which indicates the state of relative bondage that precedes the work of liberation. To be placed in a cloister is to be shut away from the world; and to be separated from the rest of the world signifies that what is actually shut away is essentially the lad's free Spirit. The Christ Spirit in itself is always free, but it assumes the burdens of apparent limitation imposed by incarnation into the human personality. This declaration is found in the gospel of St. John 1:14 (KJV), which states that Spirit or the Word became flesh, and dwelt among men, and by so doing, Man beheld his radiance as the Son of God who is full of grace and truth. The brother's age is a reference to the fact that he is young in his spiritual development, since age is used in occultism as a designation of the degree or level one has attained, and the number five is also used to indicate his representation of the Fifth Life Wave, and the five senses through which humanity experiences self-conscious awareness. Our five-sense reality is itself a cloister, since our sense of personal identity as apparently separate human beings is based on the five subtle principles of sensation. In this cloistered state of consciousness, the individual seems to perceive the manifestation of the indwelling Self in as many different parts as there are human beings. As this illusion is allowed to persist, the lad begins to delude himself into believing that he is not only separate from God, but he perceives himself as separate from his fellowman, from the many things constituting his environment, from Nature, and he therefore feels disconnected from everything. The five-sense three-dimensional consciousness, from which this delusion originates, is called *poverty*, and it explains why the Manifesto states that the lad was placed in the cloister "*by reason of his poverty*". His free God-Self, shut away in his tabernacle of flesh and limited by his five-sense consciousness, experiences a semblance of poverty. The Masters of Wisdom, who have traced human evolution, know that five-sense consciousness is not evil, and that this apparent separateness has its uses. What is evil is remaining in this state for too long.

The *Fama* continues by saying that while Brother C.R.C. was in the cloister, he learned two languages: Greek, a reference to the disciplines of philosophy and religion, and Latin, a reference to science. Moreover, he is said to have learned "*indifferently*", meaning that he learned each language with equal eagerness and achieved equal proficiency in both. Through learning these two disciplines in the cloister, the Self of the lad begins to gain the preliminary knowledge of the Laws and the meaning of what the senses report; without which it would be impossible for him to go on to receive the higher instruction, that would acquaint him with the secrets of occult science and philosophy, since this occult instruction is said to be delivered in *"Arabic"*— the language of Initiation.[8]

The first principle of those aspiring to become practical occultists is to realize the value of education. The ancient philosopher Pythagoras demanded proficiency in music, mathematics, and astronomy of all who sought his instruction, since all occult training of the proper kind is based on the foundation of science and philosophy. With this educational foundation in place, the fifteen-year-old Brother C.R.C., still earnest and desirous of his quest, reaches the next step where he comes into association with Brother P.A.L, who is determined to go to the Holy Land. It is at this age of fifteen, when adolescence sets in, that the subtle forces, symbolized by the serpent, the scorpion, and the eagle begin to stir in the bodies of boys and girls, bringing about the necessary physiological changes and mental transformation characteristic of puberty. At this time, they are stirred by a desire for adventure and new experiences, as they long for a wider horizon and to see these desires manifest. Psychologists are only now beginning to comprehend that these inner stirrings are closely related to occult and mystical experiences. The serpent power awakened at the initial stage of Initiation is, in fact, the same force that is termed *"libido"* by analytic psychologists and responsible for both the impulses and emotions connected with the perpetuation of the race of Man through reproduction, and with the liberation of Man from spiritual bondage. The quest for the reality beyond mere sensation, and the search for the truth that transcends ordinary reasoning, called mysticism and occultism, are functions of the movement of this same Scorpio energy as it awakens the centers of consciousness in the body.

The deeper occult significance of the number and age of fifteen, is the theosophical extension of the number five, which is arrived at by adding the numbers 1 through 5: $1+2+3+4+5=15$. The expansion of consciousness, which has taken Brother C.R.C. from the age of five to the age of fifteen, symbolizes the completion of his preparatory five-sense cycle of training, and his readiness to leave the cloister. Qabalists attribute the number fifteen to that aspect of reality named Wisdom, but this does not mean that Brother C.R.C. has attained this grade, it simply means that the impulse which stirs us into activity when we begin to long for something higher than five-sense experiences, is one that originates in Celestial Wisdom. On the Tree of Life, Wisdom is called "the Father", and like the Prodigal Son, this longing for the Father's House is what urged him to leave the five-sense life to make his journey back home to the Holy Land. This stage of progress reached by C.R.C, becomes evident when he speaks of Brother P.A.L. Qabalists agree that Brother P.A.L. is "the Fool", a symbol of the Life Breath in Man, working on the superconscious level, and representing the spirit in search of experience. The Fool, who is the Prince in the other world, is on his travels through this one and he corresponds to the sphere of the "Christ" or the "Son" called Tiphareth on the Tree of Life.[9]

He is seated in the heart of the human personality, and is on earth to do "the Will of the Father." With the five-sense life fulfilled, the Divine presence of the Father stirs up the superconscious life and creates in Man an earnest desire and longing to go to the "Holy Land" of super-sensuous experience. We can see that even when Brother C.R.C. was in the cloister, he like all humanity was still associated with Brother P.A.L., who represents the power of the Crown or the Primal Will, radiating from the indivisible "I AM", called the "Father." However, the essential Spirit or I AM is veiled by the outer forms of human personality. The psychological aspect of those first stirrings for higher things is related to the serpent power and the spiritual motivation that comes from the awakening of our desire, by an impulse originating in the universal and *Indivisible Self.* The indwelling Christ within the individual remains locked in the cloister of the five-sense reality, unless these eager longings are stirred. Therefore, all mystery rites agree that the *first preparation* of a candidate for initiation must be in the heart.

Jerusalem, "The Abode of Peace", is the intended destination of this journey, with the desire to visit Jerusalem typifying the longing for contentment, the hunger for rest from strife, and the quest for peace. These are, in fact, the dominant motives that drive us forward on our Path of Initiation. When Brother C.R.C. began his journey to Jerusalem, the last crusade had been abandoned more than a hundred years earlier, and Jerusalem was a place of pilgrimage to the Holy Sepulchre. That type of pilgrimage revered dead forms of the past, and is often associated with the states of mind found in those who are just beginning their quest for truth.[10] Occult students frequently make claims to Ancient Orders and exaggerate their connection to antiquity, but the truth never grows old, and provokes the question, "Why seek the living among the dead?"

The allegory continues by saying that Brother P. A. L. died at Cyprus, but this does not mean that the superconscious impulse was extinguished. According to occult interpretation and alchemical writings what is meant here, is that the superconscious impulse was transmuted into the special activity of a certain center in the body, indicated by the name, *Cyprus*.[11] Cyprus is the birthplace of the goddess Aphrodite, a Syrian goddess identified with the Great Mother and the planet Venus, where copper was mined. Alchemists therefore named this metal Venus and Qabalists associate both the planet Venus and the metal copper with the *East*. The *East* is the place of the dawn, the womb of the light, and the direction associated with the beginning of spiritual illumination. In the Masonic tradition, Freemasons travel in an easterly direction during their Lodge ritual in search of the light, and both the chair of the Master and the Pillar of Wisdom are positioned in the East, just as the alter is placed in the eastern quarter of the Christian church. Furthermore, ancient literature indicates that the Orient is the home of occult knowledge and mystical experiences. The *Fama Fraternitatis* reveals the secrets of the Microcosm to its readers, and makes reference to the Mediterranean Sea as that inner something alchemists call "our Sea", which is placed in the middle of the earthly vehicle of personality, and is defined as the inner life with islands in it. These islands or interior centers are called chakras, by the Hindus and are called metals by alchemists who name them the Sun, the Moon, and the five planets known to the ancients. They are also said to symbolize the Seven Churches of Asia Minor spoken of in the Book of Revelation. The Venus center symbolized by Cyprus is a nerve plexus in the throat of Man, which links the four lower centers in the body with the two higher centers in the head. The endocrine secretion released by the Venus center in the throat, is essential to any further development of the individual, since it stimulates the sun or heart center, located in the cardiac plexus of the upper trunk and releases a radiant energy in the body that corresponds to the radiant energy of the physical sun in the sky, which is its metaphysical counterpart.[12] The radiant energy released by the heart through the stimulation of the Venus center, must now rise to the head to be combined with the Moon and Mercury centers in the head, which correspond to the pituitary and pineal bodies respectively. There can be no beginning of true and serious occult development until Brother P.A.L., who represents the metaphysical power of the physical sun, "dies at Cyprus", which means that the super-conscious impulses received through the sun center, are changed or transmuted into the awakened functioning of the Venus center.[13] It must be noted here that Venus, planetary ruler of the throat center, and the inner and outer hearing centers in the brain, is also associated with the zodiacal sign of Taurus, known as "the Bull of Form." The arousal of emotion by the awakening the heart and throat centers is essential to the furthering of the physical and spiritual development that characterizes the evolution of the Brother, since no one can attain great spiritual heights with only an intellectual curiosity. After Brother P.A.L. dies, Brother C.R.C. continues on his journey to Jerusalem. His first impulse has been modified by the impulses from the Scorpio, heart and head centers, but he persists in his quest, with his desire for peace being his dominant motive. The journey continues in its original direction until Brother C.R.C. reaches Damascus, where he was halted for a time due to the "feebleness of his body". The term Damascus means "work", and every student of occultism soon comes to know that some purely physiological adjustments must be made; that a sound mind in a sound body is critical; and that to achieve this strength of body requires work, so some time must be spent in Damascus. While in Damascus, Brother C.R.C. gains favor with the Turks "by reason of his skill in medicine."

This makes this story intriguing because Brother C.R.C. is just a little more than fifteen years old, is a Christian, and has not studied medicine. Additionally, for a German lad to have gained favorable notice by the Mohammedans who held Christians in contempt, makes the story even more interesting.[14] The *Fama* explains that one result of the work of physical reconstruction, is the development of unusual skills in controlling bodily functions, and this requires hard work, time, and effort, which is essential for anyone preparing himself for Initiation. Any system of practice should include the establishment of a proper diet, proper use of water, rhythmic breathing, and such control of the muscles in the body, that the individual would be able to stand for an hour at a time, without moving or suffering discomfort.[15] Those who wrote the *Fama* were fully aware of the laws governing the evolution of the human, and they knew that the Turks, who are Mongolians, are the primary members of the Fourth Life Wave. So, the friendliness of the Turks to Brother C.R.C. alludes to the fact that the preliminary practices mentioned above awaken the mental and physical powers that were highly developed in the Fourth Life Wave, but had been temporarily submerged in the collective subconscious. However, the real objective of the work in Damascus is not the awakening of the Fourth Life Wave powers, because the awakening of those powers automatically comes about as a by-product of the work itself. The cleansing of the physical vehicle, which included chastity of thought, word and deed, is the reason for the training and for the work— the objective being preparation for Initiation. There are no exceptions to these requirements, and anyone who neglects to adhere to strict preparation, does so at his own peril, and may never go beyond Damascus. During these practices, the body releases very potent physical and psychical forces, which are designed to bring it under control, and unless these forces are strictly monitored, the result could be insanity, sexual perversion, and other disorders. So the importance of moderation and restraint cannot be too heavily emphasized here.

As a result of his strict training Brother C.R.C. "became acquainted with the Wise Men of Damcar in Arabia, and beheld what great wonders they wrought, and how Nature was discovered unto them."[16] This alludes to the first interior awakening of hearing and sight, which is a direct result of the function of the Venus center in the throat, whose secretions when released into the bloodstream, affect the awakening of the hearing center in the brain, and at the same time, stir up essential, deep, and genuine emotions, allowing the Brother to begin to *hear* the Wise Men. Students of the Ageless Wisdom teachings will remember that Taurus is related to inner hearing and also to the Hierophant, who is the High Priest of the Temple. Once interior hearing is developed, inner vision, which is mental, and constitutes true intuition or inner instruction, follows. Inner vision must not to be confused with clairvoyance or astral vision. True inner sight is heightened mental perception, the ability to see with the mind's eye— the kind of sight that allows the individual on this journey to be able to see the nature of the powers of a truly liberated humanity, and also to see that full liberation reveals what is hidden by the veil of outward and illusory appearances. This is the ultimate goal of the Fifth Live Wave and Eve's reason for taking humanity on this long journey into Form. The *Fama* goes on to say that this awakening begins to stir up the high and noble spirit of Brother C.R.C., and shows him the awesome possibilities, which can be developed and realized with continued work. This realization allows the Brother to become even more determined to complete the work, and to accomplish this objective, so he subjects himself to an even stricter discipline of mind and body, as indicated by the bargain for a "certain sum of money" or "coins" that he strikes with the Arabians. As mentioned previously, in alchemy, money is a symbol of one's power of activities and one's personal, physical and mental energies. Thus, in the ancient world, cattle were the universal medium of exchange, and so Brother P.A.L., the representation of the Hebrew word Aleph, meaning "Bull" or "Ox", which stands for The Fool, is the driving life force at the cellular level of the individual.

The vow of chastity taken by the Brother at this point is indicated by the name *Arabia,* which means *"sterility"*, and refers not only to sexual abstinence, but also to formal physical and mental restraints as well as discipline. The candidate for Initiation must be completely receptive, which requires that for some time he must be free from any creative activity. The mind and the body must be still, giving meaning to the scripture, *"Be still and know that I am God"*, which relates to this stage of the Great Work.[17] The definition of Qabalah is *"Reception"*, and so, it is only by bringing the personality vehicle into complete integration with the inflow of the Divine Force that the process of Initiation can occur. The Temple of Initiation is also in Arabia, where the bargain for money was struck, and this is where Brother C.R.C. meets the Wise Men. His sojourn at the temple is for a limited time only because the total sterility required in order for the candidate to pass safely through the trials of initiation is temporary, and alludes to the statement made by Jesus that some persons make themselves eunuchs "for the kingdom of heaven's sake." This temporary sterility results in the activation of tremendous physical and subtle mental reserves of life force in the body. Once Initiation is complete, one returns to a more normal way of life, in the same way that "Enoch", which means "Initiate", who walked with God, became the father of a string of offspring.

The location of the Wise Men's temple is Damcar in Arabia, and of course, there is no such geographical location. The key to the puzzle is the name Damcar, which is a combination of "*dam*" meaning blood, and "*car*" meaning lamb, resulting in the phrase "*Blood of the Lamb*", that is common to both Hebrews and Christians. Some students of the Talmud, however, interpret "*kar*" to mean ass, and therefore interpret it as *the Blood of the Ass*, referring to the animal that carried Jesus into Jerusalem. In the occult language, Gematria, the Hebrew word Damcar is spelled DMKR which translates into the number 264, the number-name of the River Jordan, IRDN, which Qabalists and alchemists associate with the "Water of Minerals", as do many esoteric interpretations of the scriptures that associate the River Jordan with the bloodstream of man.[18] The Lamb is a symbol of both Christian and Hindu study, and the process of Initiation is one in which the powers of the Christos or Christ consciousness are liberated and brought into expression within the life of the Initiate. This, in turn, brings about the perfection of the vehicle to allow for the expression of these powers through their transmission from the causal plane into the physical plane. The practices of initiation precipitate changes in the chemistry of the initiate's blood, constituting the Abode of the Wise Men in Damcar. And, like the building of Solomon's Temple, made without hands eternal in the heavens, this spiritual temple of the initiate as a vehicle of consciousness, was therefore constructed without the sound of the hammer, and is a spiritual, rather than a material building. The occult medicine and mathematics learned by Brother C.R.C. in Damcar brought about changes in the chemistry of the blood, the bones and the tissues of the initiated. In like manner, the perfection of the physical vehicle, under the mental direction of the spiritual forces in the initiated, brings about a regenerated being who is now a "citizen of heaven." The reasons we do not have more Masters of Wisdom is because of the intense work and strict discipline required as well as the laziness of humanity, who continually wastes its time and is always looking for the easy way out.[19]

When Brother C.R.C. arrives at Damcar he is sixteen years old. The relationship between his age and the symbolism of the Qabalistic Tarot Key 16, the Tower, which refers to the Tower of Babel mentioned in the Christian Bible, are evident. This Tower was constructed on a foundation of separateness, and false knowledge, symbolizing the distorted notion that there is an independent "personal will." In the imagery of the Key, a lightning bolt strikes the crown of the Tower, which represents Will and one's fundamental thinking, bringing about its overthrow, and this flash of lightning is therefore a strike that destroys the premise of separateness. Hence, at the occult age of 16, the Brother is awakened to the fundamental truth that there can be no such thing as personal independence, personal autonomy, or personal separateness. Moreover, the number sixteen, which is also the square of the number four, has always been associated with heavenly order, and with Jupiter, the wielder of the thunderbolt, who destroys the Tower of Falsehood by directing the Light from above. The conclusion here is that one absolutely cannot progress to the higher grades of Initiation with these false notions, since they preclude one's receptivity to any further training or instruction.

Now sixteen, and in Damcar, the Brother meets the Wise Men who received him, not as a stranger, but as someone they had expected, and the Fama, states here that he was also armed with "a Dutch constitution", and shown secrets out of his cloister. When the work of initiation starts, he begins to realize that he is not alone on his quest for truth because his interior mechanism is so finely attuned and awakened, that he is very receptive to the more vivid and direct contact made with the Masters of Wisdom. During this time he realizes that his occult development and progress had been under observation for many years, even before he was consciously aware of the urge to follow the Path of Return. He also gains a deeper and clearer understanding of his five-sense experiences, as many impressions stored in his subconsciousness, including recollections from previous incarnations, are brought to the surface and their meanings better understood.

It is of paramount importance to recognize that the Wise Men are actually human beings, who are members of the Third Order of the Invisible Fraternity. Let me, however, hasten to add here that this term "fraternity" is a generic one, since the *true* Fraternal Order consists of both men and women who have attained the Third Order, and are referred to as "Brothers and Sisters", not Masters. These Masters are only visible to humans, whose eyes *"have received strength borrowed from the eagle."* The *eagle* being one of the symbols for the Scorpio center that refers to the nerve force, which normally finds its outlet through the reproductive functions. On the reverse path of the aspirant this same sexual force opens up the sight center in the brain allowing the aspirant to see with the mind's eye, and with the mind of God. Therefore, no attempt should ever be made to force these centers to express outside the initiatory process. Modifications of the body through glandular secretions, which result in changes in the bloodstream and modifications of the structures in certain areas of the brain can only be achieved through the process undertaken by Brother C.R.C.[20] The Age of Pisces which has just ended has prepared human vehicles to receive the energy and light from the Sun Sirius in Aquarius, so that today we are seeing the largest number of individuals since creation, poised to consciously embark on the journey to the Holy Land as Brother C.R.C. did. The present state of human consciousness has been achieved through the work carried out by the personality and the soul in the Age of Pisces, and facilitated the development of the physical, emotional and mental bodies, thus making it possible to undertake this adventure. When the individual accomplishes the preliminary work of purifying his mind and body, when he knocks on the right door, when he asks the right questions, and when he shows himself to be duly prepared, he will be led to those who will give him the necessary instruction.

Brother C.R.C. began his work in Damcar having perfected *"the Arabian tongue"*, a kind of occult language that combines sound with meaning, and is different from the five-sense consciousness. This *"Arabian tongue"* relates to a mode of expression that is active during a period of temporary celibacy, and produces unusual insights into the secrets of nature. The Initiate is now able to put the permanent knowledge gained into an orderly fashion, thus attaining a high and profound understanding of the principles and laws on which life and nature are based. The time taken to acquire this knowledge is said by the *Fama* to be three years, but it emphasizes that a lack of commitment, desire, and discipline could extend this timeline. To become a true *"Arabian"*, one must have no other Will, but to do the Will of the One Life, which leaves no excuse for those who say that their outer life prevents them from making ready for Damcar. The work is open to all, and its treasures are offered freely to all, but ultimately only the worthy can receive the gift.[21]

All these initiatory practices at Damcar, which took Brother C.R.C. three years, were aimed at perfecting the personality, and providing a new vehicle in which the God-Self could dwell. Brother C.R.C. is now nineteen years old. The Qabalistic Tarot Key 19 is related to the Sun which is the symbol of regenerated self-consciousness, and it shows two children playing in a fairy ring with the face of the sun overhead emitting thirty-two rays—sixteen feminine, and sixteen masculine. In Hebrew nineteen is the number of Chavah, which means Eve. To the Hindus she is known as Prakriti; and in Egypt as Mother Isis, the Alchemical Woman and the Alchemical Moon who is associated with the metal Silver. On becoming a true initiate, the Candidate begins to understand that the macrocosmic manifestation of the perfect law of liberty, which proceeds from the God-Self dwelling within him at the center, is an expression of the heavenly order called "the little sister." At this stage of development, through the manifesting power of the universe, the dark, terrible Mother is transformed into the symbol of Wisdom. Nature is indeed terrible to those who do not understand her, but to the initiated and regenerated personality, she is a joyous companion in the Dance of Life. In Egypt, Isis, the symbol of Wisdom, was regarded as the Spouse and Sister of Osiris, the Father of Wisdom. Once torn off, the mask of terror reveals that this "mysterious power", is the kinswoman, who is also the beloved and the partner.

Brother C.R.C. spent his twentieth year completing the journey from Damcar to Egypt, spending some time there to finish his work. The journey to Egypt took him across *Sinus Arabicus,* the Arabian Gulf, intimating that the period of celibacy represented by Arabia was now ended. Symbolically, Egypt is the land of darkness, bondage and captivity, and the automatic region of subconsciousness, but it is also the place that everyone must go to on his journey to Jerusalem, as did Jesus, Joseph, Pythagoras and all the Masters of Wisdom. The work of the initiate in Egypt involves investigation into the modes of power developed in man during the process of his evolution from the vegetable through to the animal kingdom. Brother C.R.C.'s twentieth year in Egypt corresponds to the Tarot Key 20, which depicts the three figures representing the Egyptian triad— Osiris, Isis and Horus, rising from their coffins and sitting on universal subconsciousness, symbolized by the ocean. This image symbolizes the revival of both the God-powers of "Egypt", and the subconscious powers of the human personality. The psychic powers of 'Egypt", which reside in the region below the surface of consciousness and ordinary sensation, are unquestionably marvelous, but can become an obstacle to real advancement along the Path of Liberation. Any undertaking to explore the region described as "darkly splendid", which is associated with Hades, the Greek name for the abode of departed spirits, should not be ventured into before completing the three year training that Brother C.R.C. received, and marvels of automatic consciousness should most definitely be avoided.

The ladder of seven steps leading down to this region is the same one that the initiate, with the right occult training, must climb on his ascent up to the mountaintop of Initiation. The Masters of Wisdom warn everyone not to stoop down, nor to descend, because the ladder should always be one of ascent, since this allows for the sublimation or rising of the "Egyptian" powers.

The seven rungs of the ladder refer to the seven chakras, and to the Seven Churches of Asia. Most failures in occult development are due to the fascination of aspirants with the glamour and allures of Egypt, which lead to prolonged sojourns there, and then to intolerable slavery. Although everyone must go down into Egypt, and it is a requirement of the journey to the Holy Land, in the Bible we are admonished not to "tarry" in Egypt. For while one cannot become a Master of Wisdom without being acquainted with subhuman powers, every true teacher has an obligation to make his students aware of the pros and cons of "Egypt", to encourage their self-reliance, to encourage less reliance on authority, and to make their students unafraid.[22] With his studies of Egypt now complete, Brother C.R.C. sailed west across the Mediterranean Sea from Cyprus, where the work of transmutation had begun, to Fez in Morocco, whose location is directly opposite to Cyprus on the western end of the sea. An occult history of Fez reveals that in the fourteenth century, it was the intellectual center of the world, with a great university and a well-established library, which attracted men of learning and inquiry. Thus in this allegory, Fez corresponds to the intellectual powers associated with Hermes or Mercury, and to the powers expressed through the organs in the head of man. It is interesting to note here that the "*fez*" named after the city, and the Turkish headdress, has a direct reference to this head center. Indeed, Fez was the center for the study of the Hermetic sciences—Mathematics, Chemistry, Medicine and Alchemy, and in Fez Brother C.R.C makes the acquaintance of those who reveals many of their secrets to him. Until one has passed through the stages of physical and mental development, represented by the earlier undertakings of Brother C.R.C, studying the phenomena of the inorganic phases of life expression more often than not leads to gross error rather than to truth, because as wonderful as the study of subjects like chemistry, biology, and mathematics might be, the accumulation of facts is not wisdom.[23] And, without Brother C.R.C.'s training and development, the study of these subjects would be empty and will not yield the divinely intended results and benefits to either the individual or humanity. And so, scientists feel as if they are groping in the dark, simply because they have not applied the ancient occult principles and laws established from the foundation of the world in their work. But when he became acquainted with those at Fez, Brother C.R.C. recognized that their Cabala or occult knowledge, was contaminated with Religion, and here, religion refers not only to religious authoritarian dogma, but also to the "religion" of materialism, which always interferes with one's ability to receive truth.[24] In the area of alchemy or applied science, the black magic of advertising propaganda used in the physical, mental and emotional enslavement of men, women and children, is one of the corruptions Brother C. R.C. observed, and the persons he encountered were totally devoid of true spiritual understanding. However, the true occultist who is trained in the fundamental laws of consciousness, and Nature is no enemy of science. His examination and use of the results of the scientific investigations by chemists, biologists and physicists, allow him to separate the gold from the dross because of his elevated consciousness.

Brother C.R.C. departed the city of Fez after two years. He is now twenty-two years old, and at this point his name is changed to R.C. instead of C.R.C. True occult training develops in man the character of compassion or tenderness, which is the meaning of R.C. or *roke*, and so like Brother R. C., with the right occult training, everyone will then be able to solve the *Fama's* puzzle. Moreover, in occult mathematics, the number 22 represents the circumference of a circle and the completion of the manifestation of a cycle. Brother R.C. is now imbued with the full powers of his God-Self, and ready to manifest these powers through his regenerated and perfected personality vehicle. These powers distinguish him as sympathetic and tender, making him a member of that group of beings on earth known as the Lords of Compassion.

The twenty-two hidden paths on the Tree of Life, the twenty-two letters of the Hebrew alphabet, and the twenty-two phases of consciousness all refer to the magical occult age at which one becomes a Master of these paths, and a living embodiment of the Tree of Life, which is a glyph of the Regenerated Man.[25] When an Initiate completes his occult journey, the primary effect of the compassion and sympathy engendered by that training is to share that knowledge with humanity. However, extreme care must be taken in imparting that knowledge because the world has shown an antagonism to this secret, arcane knowledge, which is a function of its unwillingness to relinquish its accustomed opinions and prejudices. To those unenlightened members of humanity whose minds are accustomed to the narrow limits of traditional orthodoxy, whether scientific or religious, this knowledge is laughed at, mocked and viewed as folly.

The knowledge of Ageless Wisdom does change from age to age, so at this point Brother R.C. has new things to show—external evidences that validate this ancient doctrine, and always concur with the old philosophy. He found that the "*little wise men*" of many nations wanted nothing to do with these teachings, whose central thesis proposes the reformation of the arts and sciences, and correct the errors that have crept into those disciplines over time.[26]

Because the training of most exoteric scientists has led them away from their inner center to the many divisions in the fields of their environment, they have had immense difficulty understanding esoteric teachings, since these teachings always leads towards the center; not surprisingly, until scientists realize that the real focus and objective of research and study must be the inner life of man, they will continue to experience limited success in their work. True Occult Wisdom always leads away from the "many-ness" of the outer world to the unity at the heart of Being, and in fact is the real inner significance of the American motto, *E pluribus unum*, on the Great Seal of the United States, which, together with all the many other symbols, indicates the occult premise on which the country was founded.[27]

Brother R.C. is ready, at this point, to impart *accurate* indications of the trend of future events in considerable detail, thereby revealing how the present and the future can be brought into harmony with the past. This ability presents the cure for the faults of the Church and the errors of moral philosophy. When the knowledge of the Fama first appeared, many sought this knowledge as a means of acquiring material wealth, and unfortunately the same motive still exists today for most seekers. However, the *Fama* warns that none who entertain such an unworthy motive will ever be able to make contact with the True Occult Order.

The wealth gained by recipients of this occult wisdom is alchemical gold, silver and precious stones, both literally and figuratively, and, in fact, the unusual control of material supply is one of the results of occult wisdom. These men and women have been brought forth on the scene of time as repositories of this great knowledge and wisdom, to function as personalities through which the manifestations of the Cosmic Order can occur. The benefits and gifts of this process are for "kings", a term that does not apply to those who occupy earthly thrones.

An old occult symbol— the Triangle of Fire— that is mentioned in this work, relates to the symbolism of the Lamb, to the Hindu God of Fire, Agni, as well as the Great Pyramid, that the Egyptians call "The Light", and is also a Stone Emblem of the Eternal Flame. This symbol appears twice on the reverse of the Great Seal of the United States; first, as an unfinished pyramid, and then as a radiant triangle with an enclosed eye. It is an indication that the structure of the government intended by the founders of the American Republic was presented to their minds as a piece of *Egyptian Masonry*; and in this respect, it must be remembered that members of the True and Invisible Rosicrucian Order were often referred to as Fire Philosophers. In the Rosicrucian manifesto, the statement, "*brake through with all force*", which is made several times, alludes to the forcible overthrow of darkness and barbarism. Washington, Franklin, Abraham Lincoln and the writers of the Declaration of Independence, were of like mind to the writers of the *Fama,* who proclaimed that it is the right of any free people to overthrow its form of government, initially by *peaceable* means, and if that is not possible, then by force.[28] Brother R.C, now a "citizen of heaven", refrains from calling attention to his unusual knowledge, an approach that was certainly true when the *Fama* was written in 1614, since at that time mankind was being told that he was a mere worm of the dust. Today, this knowledge of the *Fama* is more commonplace, due to its gradual unveiling made possible by the advancement of consciousness, and therefore a true assessment of man's nobleness and worth is now encouraging to humanity. Some would have man believe that the whole human race is nothing more than a mere incident in a series of cosmic accidents, and many are still oppressed by the theological doctrine that Man is vile, and tainted with original sin. However, the reality is that man is not a mere inhabitant of earth who is enslaved by life's changing circumstances, but that he does, in fact, have a share in the universal government, and a dwelling place in heaven.[29]

In alluding to the perfected body of the adept, the *Fama* says that Brother R.C. built himself a fitting habitation, which brought him into the circle of the Master Builders with the likes of Hiram Abiff, and Jesus the Carpenter. In this habitation, he reflected on his journey, and digested his whole initiatory experience, with the aim of understanding its consequences. The Fama also says that he spent much of his time studying mathematics, since from occult arithmetic and geometry an initiate gains the basic knowledge needed to make "fine instruments" in his "house" or his alchemical laboratory, sometimes called the "secret vessels." These vessels are references to the seven interior metals, or stars, called *chakras*.

Subsequent to his vain enterprises, and then more productive and intelligent pursuits, five years have elapsed and Brother R.C. is now twenty-seven years old. This is a very important number in occultism because it represents the second most operative cube, the numbers 1 and 8 being the other two cubes. The cube has always symbolized the constitution of the Fraternal Order, so has the Holy of Holies in the Jewish Tabernacle, and the Heavenly City spoken of in the twenty-first chapter of the Book of Revelation. The number 27 is 3x3x3, and added together, this equals the number 9, which is the number of *Yesod*, meaning Foundation, the ninth sphere on the Tree of Life. The Rosicrucian Grade associated with *Yesod* is Theoricus or Theoreticus, and at this stage, the fundamental theory of the Great Work is explained. Aditionally, the number twenty-seven is associated with the expression "intricate speech, a riddle, and enigma", which comes from the noun ChID, *kheedaw*; it also refers to the Hebrew verb BKH, *bawkah*, whose original meaning is "to distill, to drop, or to flow in drops", which alludes to the measured outpouring of the Hermetic work. BKH also means, "to weep," thus describing the real motive of the Masters of Wisdom of the Inner School, who like God, are moved by compassion and sympathy for the errors of the unenlightened, and for those who suffer from the consequences of their errors. These Masters of Wisdom love humanity, and the world, and they work unceasingly for the regeneration, liberation, and purification of the race of man. The numbers twenty-seven and nine are both related to the Hebrew adjective ZK, *zak* which means "pure" or "clean" and is used to describe Brother C.R.'s house. So, at this stage Brother C.R. becomes the Foundation or Basis of the Fraternity and he now also formulates his idea for reforming the arts and sciences, as a definite theory for how to proceed in his work becomes clear in his mind.[30]

We now turn our attention and focus to the three co-founders of the Order. They are *Brother G.V.*, *gav*, meaning *middle* or *center*; *Brother I.A.* or AI, *ayee*, meaning *"where* and *how"*, and *Brother I.O.*, whose name has a numerical value of 80, that relates to both the letter Peh, meaning mouth, and to *Yesod*, the ninth sphere— Basis, and Foundation.

Brother G.V. stands for concentration, which facilitates the equilibrium, essential to the establishment of the true *center* or *middle* in personal consciousness. From this center of power, the radiation of consciousness is projected out into the world in the form of *Light*. In their original order, Brother I.A.'s initials are the first two words of the Hebrew language, the meaning of which is, *"Let there be Light"*, and to effectively project this Light into a definite sphere of operation, one must ask the question, "*where, and how*".

The numeric value of 80 assigned to Bother I.O.'s name refers to concentration, self-interrogation and the means by which they are expressed. Because any specific work must have as it's basis or foundation a definite form of expression, so Brother I.O.'s place in this Third Order is essential to the work of human transformation. Now that all three Brothers are out of the cloister, they represent the personification of powers of the human mind at the level of self-conscious awareness.[31]

The total value of the initials of these three Brothers is one hundred (100). The number one hundred is a square of ten, and as all Qabalists will recognize, this number also represents the ten Sephiroth, or emanations on the Tree of Life, which is the Basis of the Fraternity and from which all powers are to be sought. One humdred is also the number of KLIM, *kaleem*, meaning "vases", which is comprised of the words MDVN, *madown*, signifying "*effort or extension*", and KP, *Kaph*, "*a grasping hand.*" Kaph is also the name for Tarot Key 10— the Wheel of Fortune, a symbolic representation of the *actual* constitution of the Invisible Third Order. The three Brethren identified here as the "vase" symbolize concentration, decision, and expression. The vase is the vessel into which the God-Self of Wisdom and Power, represented by Brother C.R., pours its energy, into the human vehicle, and through this activity and process, Light is radiated and extended to humanity. This operation takes place within the body-consciousness (Q) of humanity. It should be noted that the letter Q or Qoph stands for Tarot Key 18, which represents Corporeal Intelligence (the human personality vehicle).

Together, the three Brethren established the constitution of the Order in accordance with the principle of *Kaph,* that of *concentric circles,* with its three-fold divisions, as represented by the Tarot Key 10— the Wheel of Fortune.

The Fama concurs that the sole work or profession of the Brethren is to heal the sick, and this can only be accomplished through spiritual means, by establishing in human consciousness the perfect pattern of the Heavenly Man, as represented by the Qabalistic Tree of Life, which is the Glyph of Man. When the number of Brother C.R.C.'s initials (240) is added to the sum of the three co-founder Brethren— KLIM (100), the total is 340, which is the value of ShM, the Great Name of Jehovah (IHVH), and this is the last word of the *Fama.* The number 340 is also the value of SPR, *sepher,* which means, *"Book."*

Now the Fama also states that the first work of the Brethren was the compilation of a large dictionary, which they accomplished through the creation of letters, a magical language, and writing. They began Book M, the *Liber Mundi* or SPR through their combined labors, depending on the wisdom received from Brother R.C.[32] The writing of this *"Book'* was hindered because of the help needed by so many who were "sick", which alludes to the fact that in the early stages of any occult work, the work is always hampered by the *"sickness"* of the very people it is designed to help.

At this point, the *Fama* says that Brother C.R.C.'s new building "The House of the Holy Spirit" is complete and is a very far cry from the *"neat and fitting habitation"* he had made for himself. Moreover, it is a building— *Domus Sancti Spiritus*— that shall never be visible, touched, or destroyed, by the wicked of the world.[33] Four more Brethren, representing the elements required to complete the establishment of any organized effort to communicate occult instruction, are now drawn into the work.

The first of these elements designated by the initials, R. C., *roke*, means compassion. For anyone who would serve in this work, the following basic requirements are mandatory:

- Sympathy for human suffering
- The ability to understand human problems by putting oneself in another's shoes
- The unselfish desire to lift the heavy burden of ignorance from the minds of the unenlightened

It is not enough to give money. One must have the patience and the understanding to know that hate, ignorance, stupidity, fickleness, antagonism, charlatans, impostors and trickery are all to be encountered in this work, and that forgiveness and understanding are therefore essential, even though appropriate exposure is also necessary.

The second element is represented by Brother B, a reference to the Hebrew name *Beth*, and Tarot Key 1—the Magician, symbolizing Hermes and Mercury, which connects the Will or the Crown to Understanding on the Tree of Life. For alchemists, *Mercury* is the active agent in the operation of the Great Work, i.e. the work of the Sun and the Moon, and this work cannot be achieved without His aid. Brother B is also very skilled as a painter and in the use of color, which is why alchemists refer to him as their *coloring agent*. The number 1 represents the power of initiation, and is the first letter, of the first Hebrew word in Genesis. This initiative power is vital to the communication of occult instruction, since one must have passion, a strong initiative, the ability to make definite plans, and the ability to communicate the subject in proper "*colo*rs." A dull, cold, and abstract presentation of bare principles can neither capture nor hold the attention of the listener, and it is for this reason that Jesus spoke in parables.[34]

Brother G.G., *gawg*, which means, "*roof*", provides the third element needed to establish and communicate the work. His name intimates "*shelter* and *secrecy*", and he is the doorkeeper of a Masonic Lodge, who carries the name "*tiler.*" In a lodge, the function of the tiler is to make sure that only those who have the right to enter are admitted. He represents prudence and the principle of secrecy, which is necessary to ensure that true occultism, is successfully disseminated. Most of humanity resents the fact that occult knowledge is being hidden from them, but the truth is this: On the one hand, this is due to the inability of their unprepared minds to grasp the real meaning of occult doctrine; and on the other hand, the custodians of the knowledge have a responsibility to keep this information from the unprepared, through an act of mercy. Mere eagerness does not constitute *readiness to understand,* as was exemplified by Jesus, who although he spoke to the multitudes in spellbinding, verbal, moving images, reserved for a tested few, the subtler meanings of his colorful and brilliant discourses.[35]

Brother P.D. is the fourth and final one to join the group. P refers to Peh, to Mars, *the mouth*; and D, to Daleth, *the door*, and to Venus. This symbolism takes us full circle to the original idea of the whole treatise of "Unveiling the Secrets of the Feminine Principle", which is to explain the relationship of the Masculine and the Feminine Principles, and their inextricable link to each other. They are not two, but are indeed One, because the Masculine is the Feminine, and the Feminine is the Masculine. The combined values of the letters Peh, and Daleth give us the name that refers to "*the initiate*", to Enoch, the Patriarch who walked with God, and *"to be silent"*, which reminds us of the last and strongest of the four elements: *"To Know"*, *"To Will"*, *"To Dare"*, and *"To Be Silent."* Through Mars, who is related to *action*, and Venus to *communication,* we come to know that silent actions always speak louder than words. Brother P.D. is the secretary, who receives letters and applications, and is therefore the one who communicates the responses of the Fraternity. He is the Keeper of the records and understands the problems of others. He has the gift of expression, possesses imagination, and can be a mouthpiece for all. He is a true initiate, who walks with God like Enoch did. He is always silent before enemies of the work, in the face of criticism, in the presence of the unprepared, and in the most difficult situation of all, when the silly ignorance of others may tempt him to speak, even when he knows speaking is of no good consequence.

The total of all the initials is eight, which is the number of Hermes, Krishna, and the Christ. The number eight is also the number of the points bounding a cube, and reminds us of the cubical Holy of Holies, and the New Jerusalem. The total value of the initials of the eight founders is 432, which is the value of Belteshazzar, the Babylonian name of the prophet Daniel—the close connection between the prophecies of Daniel and the Book of Revelation will be revealed by a study of the Rosicrucian tenets. Once the preparatory work was completed, the Brother went out into the world as an Initiate, to serve humanity, which is one of the primary purposes for which Initiation is taken in the first place.

When both the individual and mankind achieve the Divine Marriage in Initiation, and when the lust of the Feminine for the Divine Masculine results in the absolute end of separation in the mind, Eve will finally be vindicated. Man will then know the purpose and glory for which Eve took humanity on the journey of self-discovery and knowledge.

And so, the sign of the Virgin Mother, Virgo, who symbolizes depth, darkness, quietness and warmth, becomes the valley of deep experience where secrets are discovered and eventually brought to light. This is the place where gentle, yet powerful crises and periodic developments take place in darkness, but do lead to the light. Virgo stands for the *womb of time*, the place where God's plan, which is the mystery and secret of the ages slowly matures through pain and discomfort, and in the end, through struggle and conflict brings humanity into the New Age, at the appointed time. She has brought us safely into the New Age of Aquarius, an age of a new consciousness, of a new civilization and of a new culture. Since the Mother's goal for humanity is to bring him to Christ consciousness, the sign of Virgo—the Virgin Mother— most accurately embodies the truth of this mission, which is *"Christ in you, the hope of glory."*[36]

The symbol for the New Age of Aquarius is that of the Divine Mother in the form of Isis, who is associated with the emotional nature of man. She brings subconsciousness or the underworld up to full self-conscious awareness, positioning the Feminine, as it relates to the woman or as it functions within the male, into equal expression with its counterpart, like the sun at midday in its full glory. This can only be achieved when the masculine and the feminine aspects of the individual are given full and equal authority, as is their right. In the Age of Aquarius, Isis, custodian of the long held ancient secrets, and the mysteries of Egypt, which represents the subconscious, is now the revealer of those secrets. She is the Woman spoken of in the Book of Revelation, who fully expresses her power and the proper place she occupies in the human psyche, which will be fully understood in this Age. Her revelations are the mysteries of the heart, which are of the Sun. By uniting the mind with the heart, her third aspect is able to *"earth"*, this knowledge into the physical cells and bodies of humanity for full "body-knowingness." She is described most adequately by the inscription atop the temple to Isis, at Sais:

> I, Isis am all that has been, that is, or shall be; no mortal man hath ever me unveiled. The fruit, which I have brought forth, is "the Sun."
>
> I am Isis, mistress of the whole land; I was instructed by Hermes and with Hermes, I invented the writings of the nations, in order that not all should write with the same letters. I gave mankind their laws, and ordained what no one can alter. I am the eldest daughter of Kronos; I am the wife and sister of the King Osiris. I am she who rises in the Dog-star. I am she who is called the goddess of women. I am she who separated the heaven from the earth. I have pointed out their paths to the stars. I have invented seamanship. I have brought together men and women. I have ordained that the elders shall be beloved by the children. With my brother, Osiris, I made an end to cannibalism. I have instructed mankind in the mysteries. I have taught reverence of the divine statues. I have established the temple precincts. I have overthrown the dominion of the tyrants. I have caused men to love woman. I have made justice more powerful than silver than gold. I have caused truth to be considered beautiful.[37]
>
> (Erman's Handbook of Egyptian Religion)

The third aspect of the Virgin Mother—Mary, is a symbol of the physical, and is described as *"The Mother of the Corner Stone."* She completes the work undertaken by Eve and Isis into the blood, tissue, and bones of humanity, so that Man becomes a living Stone. Mankind will come to understand in this Age that the earthly Philosopher's Stone is the true image of the real heavenly Stone, Jesus the Christ, who is the Way-Shower to Man of who he will become. Mary removes the stone or hindrance to humanity's resurrection from its spiritual death, which is a result of ignorance, by making the physical body able to receive the Divine knowledge in the cells—establishing Corporal Intelligence, and thereby transforming the candidate in preparation for Initiation. Mary, that woman of sorrow, of experience, and of aspiration, is ever the symbolism of materialism. Humanity, who is materialistic, suffering, and facing the future with despair, is still aspiring, and must emerge out of the cave of matter, forever seeking the Christ, though at first not recognizing the work he has done. And the church, the symbolic body of Christ, must purify itself of materialism, of its emphasis on theological concepts, and of its quest for political power and possession. It must remove its focus from stone buildings, and stop neglecting *"the Temple of God, not made with hands, eternal in the heavens."* Like Mary, the church must go forth to seek, the risen Christ, who it has never truly recognized.[38]

So, the return journey taken by the aspirant across the desert, from the West back to the East, is a mental, emotional and physical one. However, the Divine Mother in her three aspects—Eve, Isis, and Mary, works as the One Feminine and Creative Principle to provide the necessary conditions, on all levels, that will bring humanity back into union with the Father, with whom She is One and the same.

Afterword

We live in a world seemingly filled with turmoil, where no good options appear to exist for the majority of humanity who are trying to seek out an existence on this beautiful Emerald Isle, created by the Divine Mother for all her children to live in peace and prosperity.

We constantly hear that the rich are getting richer and the poor are getting poorer. That statement is now a bit outdated because it refers to the Age we have just left, in which the accumulation of material wealth was the primary focus. While some were gathering things of flesh, others however were gathering things of the spirit, with those who gathered things of the spirit seeming to have nothing to show for their hard labor. But, Ageless Wisdom has always reminded us that nothing is ever what it appears to be. Therefore, since this Age of Aquarius is the Age of Spirit, I am sure that their spiritual riches will become more and more evident.

The physical needs of humanity attest to the spiritual poverty of most of those who have acquired material wealth. But, once the heart and the mind are open to the Sun, no one endowed with the riches of the Kingdom of Heaven, can look aside while his brothers and sisters languish in material poverty and physical pain. No one can be free unless his brother is also free. Each is essential to the other. The rich need their seemingly materially poor brothers, because without them, the ability to be compassionate cannot be evoked, and their hearts remain closed. Likewise, the materially poor need the materially rich to help them realize their ability to receive, and this in turn give their hearts the ability to open. Mankind needs his Black, his Jewish, his Islamic, his White, his Female, his Brother, his Sister, the Sinner and the Saint to show him the way home.

The Red man, the Yellow man, and the Blue man all hold keys to the liberation of each other, and it is only in the merging of these three that the sevenfold nature of man can be expressed as *true* whiteness, the symbol of Absolute Unity.

The White Sun is the symbol for Uranus, the ruler of the Age of Aquarius, and under its influence we will see the synthesis of the Red Sun, and the Blue Moon. Then, with the aid of the Golden Sun, which symbolizes the consciousness of the Christ, who the Greeks call Hermes and the Romans call Mercury, we will see the Violet energy of Aquarius come into full bloom and establish the Age of the Brotherhood of Man—the Age of Synthesis.

It is incumbent on the daughters of Isis to wake up and remember their obligation to themselves and to humanity. They must assume their rightful position of equal rulership with their brothers, for without this the liberation of humanity from the bondage of ignorance will be further delayed.

References

Chapter One

[1]Haich, Elisabeth: *Initiation*, London: George Allen and Unwin Ltd., 1965, pg. 174.

[2]Ibid. p. 172

[3]Ibid. p. 175

[4]Ibid. p. 176

[5]Blavatsky, H. P., *Isis Unveiled*, vol.1, Pasadena: Theosophical University Press, CA, 1960, p. 301

[6]Ibid. p. 303

[7]Ibid. p. 303

Chapter Two

[1]Hall, Manly Palmer, *The Secret Teachings of All Ages*, Los Angeles: The Philosophical Research Society, p. 302.

[2]Ibid. p. 303

[3]Haich, Elisabeth: *Initiation*, London: George Allen and Unwin Ltd., 1965, p. 174

[4]Ibid, p. 230

[5]Ibid, p. 231

[6]Lawlor, Robert, *Sacred Geometry*, London: Thames and Hudson Ltd., 1982, p. 23

[7]Ibid, p. 35

[8]Case, Paul Foster, *The True and Invisible Rosicrucian Order*, Los Angeles: Builders of the Adytum Ltd., 1989, p. 47

[9]Ibid, p. 48

[10]Lawlor, Robert, *Sacred Geometry*, London: Thames and Hudson Ltd., 1982, p. 35.

[11]Prasad, Rama, *Nature's Finer Forces*, Theosophical Publishing Society, London, 1894, p. 28

[12]Lawlor, Robert, *Sacred Geometry*, London: Thames and Hudson Ltd., 1982, p. 20

[13]Ibid. p. 20

[14]Ibid. p. 56

[15]Case, Paul Foster, *The True and Invisible Rosicrucian Order*, Los Angeles: Builders of the Adytum Ltd., 1989, p. 117

[16]Ibid, p. 118

[17]Lawlor, Robert, *Sacred Geometry*, London: Thames and Hudson Ltd., 1982, p. 71

[18]Case, Paul Foster, *The True and Invisible Rosicrucian Order*, Los Angeles: Builders of the Adytum Ltd., 1989, p. 49

Chapter Three

[1]Bailey, Alice A., *A Treatise On White Magic*, London: Lucis Publishing Compamy, 1934, p. 500

[2] Bailey, Alice A., *Esoteric Astrology*, London: Lucis Publishing Company, 1951, p.10-11

[3] Bailey, Alice A., *A Treatise On Cosmic Fire*, London: Lucis Publishing Company, 1925, p. 479

[4]Ibid p. 926

[5]Ibid p. 931

[6]Ibid p. 931

[7]Ibid p. 559

[8]Ibid p. 516

[9]Ibid p. 19-20

[10]Bailey, Alice A., *Esoteric Astrology*, London: Lucis Publishing Company, 1951, p.559.

[11]Ibid p. 130

[12]Bailey, Alice A., *A Treatise On Cosmic Fire*, London: Lucis Publishing Company, 1925, pp. 83-84

[13]Bailey, Alice A., *A Treatise On White Magic,* London: Lucis Publishing Company, 1934, p. 502

[14]Bailey, Alice A., *Esoteric Astrology*, London: Lucis Publishing Company, 1951, p.168

[15]Blavatsky, H. P., *Secret Doctrine*, vol. 1, Pasadena: Theosophical University Press, 1970, p. 83

Chapter Four

[1]*The Emerald Tablet of Hermes,* p. v

[2]Boehme, Jacob, *Mysterium Magnum*, London: M. Simmons, 1653, p. 432

[3]Blavatsky, H. P., *Isis Unveiled*, Pasadena: Theosophical University Press, 1970, p. 133

[4]Toward, Thomas, *The Creative Process in the Individual*, New York: Dodd, Mead and Company, 1944, p. 109

[5]Bailey, Alice A., *Esoteric Astrology*, London: Lucis Trust Company, 1951, p. 318

[6]Atwood, M. A., *The Hermetic Philosophy and Alchemy*, New York: The Julian Press, 1960, p. 344.

[7]Case, Paul F., Case, Paul Foster, *The True and Invisible Rosicrucian Order*, Los Angeles: Builders of the Adytum Ltd., 1989, p. 58

[8]Hall, Manly P., *Man, the Grand Symbol of the Universe*, New York: Macoy Publishing and Masonic Supply Company, 1957, pp. 163,169

[9]Case, Paul F., Case, Paul Foster, *The True and Invisible Rosicrucian Order*, Los Angeles: Builders of the Adytum Ltd., 1989, p. 49

[10]Bailey, Alice A., *Treatise on Cosmic Fire*, London: Lucis Trust Company, 1951, pp. 899-900

Chapter Five

[1]Bailey, Alice A., *Esoteric Astrology*, London: Lucis Publishing Company, 1951, p. 657

[2]Besant, Annie, *The Seven Principles of Man*, London: The Theosophical Publishing House Ltd., 1943, p. 6

[3] Bailey, Alice A., *Esoteric Astrology*, London: Lucis Publishing Company, 1951, p.11

[4]Three Initiates, *The Kybalion*, Chicago, The Yogi Publication Society, Masonic Temple, 1940, pp. 26, 27

[5]Ibid p. 29

[6]Ibid p. 30

[7]Ibid p. 32

[8]Ibid p. 35

[9]Ibid p. 38

[10]Ibid pp. 39-40

[11]Case, Paul Foster, *The True and Invisible Rosicrucian Order*, Maine: Samuel Wiser, Inc., 1985, p. 128

[12]Bailey, Alice A., *Esoteric Astrology*, London: Lucis Publishing Company, 1951, p. 281

[13] Case, Paul, *The True and Invisible Rosicrucian Order*, Maine, Samuel Wiser, Inc., 1985, pp. 70-71.

[14]Ibid pp. 109-110

[15]Bailey, Alice A., *Esoteric Astrology*, London: Lucis Publishing Company, 1951, p. 357

[16]Ibid p. 272

[17]Ibid p. 263

[18]Ibid p. 149

[19]Bailey, Alice A., *Initiation Human and Solar*, London: Lucis Publishing Company, 1951, p. 206

[20]Bailey, Alice A., *Light of the Soul*, London: Lucis Publishing Company, 1951, pp. 302,303

[21]Bailey, Alice A., *Esoteric Astrology*, London: Lucis Publishing Company, 1951, pp. 138,139

[22]Case, Paul Foster, *The True and Invisible Rosicrucian Order*, Maine: Samuel Wiser, Inc., 1985, p. 300

[23]Pryse, James M., *The Restored New Testament*, London: John K. Watkins, 1914, p.319

[24] Case, Paul Foster, *The True and Invisible Rosicrucian Order*, Maine: Samuel Wiser, Inc., 1985, p. 131

[25]Ibid p. 172

[26]Ibid p. 173

[27]Bailey, Alice A., *Esoteric Psychology*, Volume 1, London: Lucis Publishing Company, 1951, pp. 292,293

[28]Ibid pp. 292,293

[29]Ibid p. 264

[30]Ibid p. 660

[31]Ibid p.195

[32]Case, Paul Foster, *The True and Invisible Rosicrucian Order*, Maine: Samuel Wiser, Inc., 1985, p. 244

[33] Bailey, Alice A., *Esoteric Astrology*: London: Lucis Publishing Company, 1951, p.143

[34]Case, Paul Foster, *The True and Invisible Rosicrucian Order*, Maine: Samuel Wiser, Inc.,1985, p. 255

[35]Bailey, Alice A., *Esoteric Astrology*: London, Lucis Publishing Company, 1951, p. 294

[36]Ibid p. 16, 17

[37]Ibid p. 559

[38]Ibid p. 154

[39]Ibid p. 559

[40]Case, Paul Foster, *The True and Invisible Rosicrucian Order*, Maine: Samuel Wiser, Inc., 1985, p. 179

[41]Bailey, Alice A, *The Light of the Soul*, London: Lucis Publishing Company, 1951, pp.173,176

[42]Ibid pp. 173,176

[43]Ibid pp. 173,176

[44]Ibid pp. 173,176

[45]Ibid pp. 174, 177

[46]Ibid pp. 174,177

[47]Ibid pp. 175,177

Chapter Six

[1]Hall, Manly P., *Man, the Grand Symbol of the Mysteries*, Los Angeles: The Philosophical Research Society, 1972, p. 154

[2]Ibid p. 156

[3]Bailey, Alice A., *A Treatise on Cosmic Fire*, London: Lucis Publishing Company, 1951, p. 685

[4] Hall, Manly P., *Man, the Grand Symbol of the Mysteries*, Los Angeles: The Philosophical Research Society, 1972, p. 158

[5]Ibid p.161

[6]Case, Paul Foster, *The True and Invisible Rosicrucian Order*, Maine: Samuel Weiser, Inc., 1989, p. 102

[7] Hall, Manly P., *The Secret Teachings of All Ages*, Los Angeles: The Philosophical Research Society, 1972, p. *LI*

[8] Bailey, Alice A., *Esoteric Astrology*, London: Lucis Publishing Company, 1951, p. 309

[9] Bailey, Alice A., *Initiation Human and Solar*, London: Lucis Publishing Company, 1951, p. 127

[10] Bailey, Alice A., *Esoteric Astrology*, London: Lucis Publishing Company, 1951, p. 196

[11]Case, Paul Foster, *The True and Invisible Rosicrucian Order*, Maine: Samuel Weiser, Inc., 1989, p. 257

[12]Bailey, Alice A., *Esoteric Astrology*, London: Lucis Publishing Company, 1951, p. 230

[13]Ibid p. 288

[14]Ibid p. 586

[15]Ibid p. 350

[16]Ibid p. 300

[17]Case, Paul Foster, *The True and Invisible Rosicrucian Order*, Maine: Samuel Weiser, Inc., 1989, p.70

[18]Ibid. p. 138

[19]Levi, Eliphas, *The Mysteries of Magic*, London: Kegan, Paul, Trench, Trubner and Company, 1897, p. 292

Chapter Seven

[1]Waite, A. E., *The Holy Kabbalah, the Higher Secret Doctrine*, New York: University Books, New Hyde Park, p. 342

[2]Ibid p. 345

[3]Ibid p. 344

[4]Ibid p. 349

[5]Ibid p. 347

[6]Ibid p. 353

[7]Ibid p. 365

[8]Ibid p. 371

[9]Ibid p. 372

[10]Ibid p. 373

[11]Ibid p. 381

[12]Ibid p. 382

[13]Ibid p. 388

[14]Ibid p. 389

[15]Ibid p. 399

[16]Ibid p. 404

[17]Ibid p. 405

[18]Case, Paul Foster, *The True and Invisible Rosicrucian Order*, Maine: Samuel Wiser, Inc., 1989, p. 183

Chapter Eight

[1]Bailey, Alice A., *Esoteric Astrology*, London: Lucis Publishing Company, 1951, p. 251

[2]Hall, Manly P., *The Secret Teachings On All Ages*, Los Angeles, The Philosophical Research Society, 1962, p. CXXVIII

[3]Blavatsky, H. P., *Secret Doctrine, vol.II*, London: The Theosophical Publishing Company, 1888, p. 410

[4]Bailey, Alice A., *Externalization of the Hierarchy*, London: Lucis Publishing Company, 1951, p. 124

[5]Case, Paul Foster, *The True and Invisible Rosicrucian Order*, Maine: Samuel Wiser, Inc., 1989, p. 63

[6]Bailey, Alice A., *Externalization of the Hierarchy*, London: Lucis Publishing Company, 1951, p. 432

[7]Case, Paul Foster, *The True and Invisible Rosicrucian Order*, Maine: Samuel Wiser, Inc., 1989, p. 3

[8]Ibid p. 66

[9]Ibid p. 68

[10]Ibid p. 69

[11]Ibid p. 69

[12]Ibid, p. 70

[13]Ibid, p. 71

[14]Ibid p. 71

[15]Ibid p. 72

[16]Ibid p. 72

[17]Ibid p. 73

[18]Ibid p. 75

[19]Ibid p. 76

[20]Ibid p. 77

[21]Ibid p. 78

[22]Ibid p. 81

[23]Ibid p. 83

[24]Ibid p. 84

[25]Ibid p. 85

[26]Ibid p. 86

[27]Ibid p. 87

[28]Ibid p. 88

[29]Ibid p. 89

[30]Ibid p. 90

[31]Ibid p. 90

[32]Ibid p. 92

[33]Ibid p. 93

[34]Ibid p. 94

[35]Ibid p. 95

[36]Bailey, Alice A., *Externalization of the Hierarchy*, London: Lucis Publishing Company, 1951, p. 252

[37]Hall, Manly P., *The Secret Teachings On All Ages*, Los Angeles, The Philosophical Research Society, 1962, p. XLV

[38]Bailey, Alice A., *Externalization of the Hierarchy*, London: Lucis Publishing Company, 1951, p. 471

Selected Bibliography

Atwood, M. A., *The Hermetic Philosophy and Alchemy*, New York: The Julian Press, 1960

Bailey, Alice A., *Esoteric Astrology*, London: Lucis Publishing Company, 1951

_____, *Externalization of the Hierarchy*, London: Lucis Publishing Company, 1951

_____, *Initiation, Human and Solar*, London: Lucis Publishing Company, 1951

_____, *Light of the Soul*, London: Lucis Publishing Company, 1951

_____, *A Treatise On Cosmic Fire*, London: Lucis Publishing Company, 1951

_____, *A Treatise On White Magic*, London: Lucis Publishing Company, 1951

Besant, Annie, *The Seven Principles of Man*, London: The Theosophical Publishing House Ltd., 1943

Blavatsky, H. P., *Isis Unveiled*, Pasadena: Theosophical University Press, 1970

_____, *The Secret Doctrine*, volumes i and ii, Pasadena: Theosophical
University Press, 1970

Boehme, Jacob, *Mysterium Magnum*, London: M. Simmons, 1653

Case, Paul Foster, *The True and Invisible Rosicrucian Order*, Los Angeles: Builders of the Adytum, Ltd., 1989

Haich, Elisabeth, *Initiation*, London: George Allen and Unwin Ltd., 1965

Hall, Manly P., *The Secret Teachings of All Ages*, Los Angeles: The Philosophical Research Society, 1962

_____, Man, the Grand Symbol of the Universe, New York: Macoy Publishing and Masonic Supply Company, 1957

Lawlor, Robert, *Sacred Geometry*, London: Thames and Hudson, 1982

Levi, Eliphas, *The Mysteries of Magic*, London: Kegan, Paul, Trench, Trubner and Company, 1897

Pyrse, James M., *The Restored New Testament*, London: John K. Watkins, 1914

Three Initiates, The Kybalion, Chicago: The Yogi Publication Society, Masonic Temple, 1940

Troward, Thomas, *The Creative Process in the Individual*, New York: Dodd, Mead and Company, 1944

Glossary of Terms

Abode of Peace: Jerusalem. The place for which, humanity hungers for rest, from strife.

Active
Intelligence: The Third of the Divine Triad called Understanding, and assigned to Binah on the Tree of Life.

Adam: A prototype of Christ; representative of the idea or pattern of the material universe designated as Eve; androgynous; a species and not a man.

Adam Kadmon: the regenerated man that the fully lighted Tree of Life depicts; the Heavenly Man; the likeness of God.

Adept: a human being who has traveled the path of evolution and has attained the final stage on the Path of Initiation. He has passed into the fifth kingdom and is now God-Man.

Agni: The Lord of Fire; the three Fires are: Electric Fire, Solar Fire, and Fire by Friction. The three aspects of Fire are: Creative Fire, Preserving Fire and the Destroyer Fire.

Akasha	the third sphere of the supernal triangle out of which the idea for the manifestation of Spirit into matter emanated. It is called the mixing bowl for the colors and vibrations present in form.
Alchemical Child:	Horus; a widow's Son and leading figure in old Egyptian religion; the son of Osiris and Isis.
Alchemical Woman:	Isis; the Mother to whom the elements of: Fire, Water, Air, and Earth are assigned
Alchemy:	an Egyptian Art, given to the world by Hermes Trismegistus; the process by which based metal is turned to silver and gold in the cauldron that is the human body in which the process of transmutation takes place by fire and water, with the aid of air, the mind. The process is the evolution of consciousness.
Androgyne:	the One undifferentiated Intelligence before separation into its negative and positive polarities.
Apas:	one of the five Twattas that represents the element of water.
Apocalypse:	a Qabalistic book exactly indicated by the numbers and figures of the Urim, Thummim, Teraphim, and Ephod; an epitome of the Universal Mystery.
Aquarian Age:	the next 2,500-year period in which humanity will bring about the spiritualization of matter, and the occult teachings will be externalized and made more available to the

masses; Age in which the Mystery of the Feminine will be revealed

Arabic: The language of Initiation according to the *Fama Fraternitatis.*

Aryan: members of the Fifth Root Race, or Fifth Life Wave, represented by the seven churches of Asia Minor: the Arch-Indian branch; the Arch-Persians; the Chaldean-Egyptian-Semetic; the Grecian-Latin-Roman; the Teuton-Anglo-Saxon; the Slavic; and the Manichean.

Aspect, third: the sphere of Understanding assigned to the Divine Mother.

Ascended Master: one who has traveled the road of illumination and achieved Illumination; s/he is now a member of the Hierarchy who serves in the liberation of humanity.

Astrology: the science of the relationships that exist between all living organisms within the universe.

Atlanteans: inhabitants of Atlantis, who were the Fourth Root Race, or Fourth Life Wave.

Atlantis: the continent that followed the Lemurian civilization; it was located, according to Plato, in the Atlantic Ocean and was home of the Fourth Root Race, or Fourth Life Wave, called the Atlanteans.

Babel, Tower of: an occult symbol of separation, built on a foundation of false knowledge and delusion.

Builders, listening: the devas who pick up that particular note, and tone from the transmitters of the physical

	plane sound, which is needed to gather the substance for any intended material form.
Camel:	refers to the Hebrew name Gimel; a symbol of transportation, commerce, and that which unites one point in space with others and carries news from one place to another; ship of the desert.
Cardinal Cross:	The Cross of the Risen Christ; concerns "the beginning of the endless Way of Revelation."
Chakras:	seven primary vortices, or wheels of energy that work in association with the endocrine glands in man's physical, emotional, and mental bodies toward his total development.
Christ Consciousness:	that stage in man's evolution where duality ends.
Churches, Seven of Asia Minor:	symbolic of the seven branches of the Aryan race; they are: Ephesus; Smyrna; Pergamos; Thyatira; Sardia; Philadelphia; Laodicea.
Consciousness:	the responses and reactions of the individual to the forces of the twelve constellations and the twelve planets impacting him. This leads to the development of the life of the soul toward the will-to-power, the will-to-love, and the will-to-know.
Cosmic Order:	relating to a consciousness that is beyond the planetary scheme, and to the individuals who have attained this level of consciousness working on both the planetary and universal levels of the divine plan

C.R.C, Brother:	the name of the chief of German nobility who undertook the journey through the desert and arrived in Jerusalem— the Abode of Peace.
Cube:	symbolic representation of the Holy of Holies, and the New Jerusalem; one of the five Platonic or Pythagorean solids with six squares as faces.
Cyprus:	the fabled birthplace of a Syrian goddess, and where a great center to Venus is erected; associated with a nerve plexus in man's throat; a place where copper is mined and where Brother P.A.L. dies.
Daleth:	the Hebrew name for the Empress, or Venus.
Devil:	the veiled aspect of Archangel Michael; the mental creation of mankind; the repository of mankind's fears and ignorance.
Dissolution:	A secret of the Great Work; primarily a psychological process, which lifts up the energy stored in the subconsciousness into the field of conscious awareness; changes in the physical and subtle bodies of the alchemist.
Dodecahedron:	one of the five Platonic or Pythagorean solids with twelve regular pentagons as faces.
Eagle:	one of the symbols for the sign of Scorpio, whose force brings about subtle changes in the body, bringing about the beginning of the process of initiation.

Unveiling the Secrets of the Feminine Principle

Elementals, seeing:	they take the materials gathered by the *listening elementals,* and build any specific form.
Elohim:	She who is God; the Feminine aspect of Jehovah Elohim; its Qabalistic value is seven.
Emanations:	the ten outward expressions of the, "One about which naught can be said." These are called Sephiroth on the Tree of Life.
Endocrine glands:	seven ductless glands generally aligned with the spine and are associated with the seven vortices of energy called chakras. They play a vital role in the evolution of man.
Enlightenment:	the synthesis of instinct, intellect and intuition in the Pilgrim brought about by mental unfoldment, which produces in the aspirant, the final stage of mental evolution along the Path of Initiation.
Enoch:	the name of the patriarch who walked with God, and signifies "initiate"; is also associated with Hermes Trismegistus.
Esoteric:	that which pertains to the knowledge and study of the energies and forces which affect the consciousness aspect of the human being, and is concerned with the soul.
Ether:	the spiritual essence of each and all of the four elements.
Etheric Body:	a web of light surrounding all bodies, and provides the scaffolding on which the physical body is built.
Exoteric:	knowledge and study of the personality.

Eve:	symbol of the mental aspect and the mind of man; attracted by the lure of knowledge to be gained through the experience of incarnation.
Evil:	separation; the veil of terror hiding the beautiful countenance of truth.
Evolution:	the inter-relation between God and his creation, cause and effect, spirit and matter; the transformation that results from divine attraction. The aims of the process being, to shield, nurture and reveal the hidden spiritual reality which veils form.
Fama Fraternitatis:	the first Rosicrucian Manifesto issued as a manuscript and circulated among German occultists ca.1610.
Fez:	a fourteenth century intellectual center of the world in Morrocco; one of the stops on Brother C.R.C.'s journey to the Holy Land.
Fifth Principle:	the principle of mind; that faculty in man, which is the intelligent thinking principle that differentiates man from the animals.
Freemasonry:	that brotherhood to which every member of the human family belongs; the largest organization in the world, and prepares candidates for the inward life.
Ganglia:	a network of nerve cells, acting as a center of nervous influence.
Garden of Eden:	the three upper worlds of Atziluth, Briah, and Yetzirah; after the *Fall*, Man descended into the fourth world of substance, called Assiah.

Germanic Nobility: the status of the German Brother C.R.C. who though of such high financial and social standing was considered to be in poverty.

Germanic People: were among the group, which helped to root the beginnings of the Fifth Life Wave, or the Fifth Root Race, called the Aryan Race on our planet. The Aryan Race consists of all seven branches of human race; *see Aryan*

God-Man: the liberated man in whom the personality and the soul are fused, and is conditioned by the divine plan, and its purpose.

Golden Section: the division of a quantity that relates its lesser part to its greater part, as the greater part is to the whole; the proportion 5:8 is the nearest arithmetic expression of this; also called the Extreme Mean Ratio.

Grace: that by which Supreme attainment is bestowed; divine favor; Shekinah is Divine Grace.

Great Bear, the: the constellation influencing the first emanation of the Divine Triad, which contained the Divine Idea of the plan to be carried out in matter. The seven brothers issue from this sphere.

Great Work, the: the process by which the merging of the personality and the soul takes place; the occultists say that this Work is accomplished by the Sun and the Moon, with the aid of Mercury.

Heart Sun, the: influences Soul consciousness; the real sun under which our planetary life is now functioning, and response is now being made.

Hercules: the journey of the Sun through the twelve signs of the zodiac and have come to be known as the Labours of Hercules.

Hermes Trismegistus: the Thrice Great who is the messenger of the gods to man, and is said to have brought writing, medicine and civilization to Earth; He embodies in himself both aspects of the mental principle; the expression of the concrete and the abstract mind of God.

Hierarchy, the: a group of spiritual beings on the inner planes of the solar system who control the evolutionary process. They are divided into twelve hierarchies. A reflection of this Hierarchy is called the occult hierarchy and is made up of adepts and initiates who are in human form.

High Priestess: the Uniting Intelligence; the Female Elder of the Temple; the thirteenth Path on the Tree of Life connecting Tiphareth with the Crown.

Hiram Abiff: the symbol of Masonry representing the Master-Builder and Grandmaster entrusted with the building of Solomon's Temple; He is the symbolic embodiment of the Lost Word; he has the Light and is, therefore, the Triune Self and the four elements combined; his life, death, and resurrection illustrates the story of Masonry and the destiny of humanity; He is the Master Mason who is symbolic of both Hermes and Jesus.

Holy of Holies: an adytum for the Indwelling Divinity; a true House of the Holy Spirit.

Holy Spirit: the third aspect of the Divine Trinity; the Shekinah; the Divine Mother

Horus: a Widow's Son; the son of Osiris and Isis; name relates to the Christ.

Human Vehicle: the personality, composed of the physical, emotional, and mental bodies.

Icosahedron: one of the five Platonic solids or Pythagorean solid with twenty equilateral triangles as faces.

Illumination: the synthesis of instinct, intellect and intuition in the Pilgrim, brought about by mental unfoldment, which produces in him the final stage of mental evolution along the Path of Initiation.

Initiate: he is the man/woman in whom there is an absence of dualism. He can stand at the center of the transforming will and bring about the needed changes in the form of nature without identifying himself with it or being affected by it. His number is eleven and he works in the eleventh sign of the zodiac, Aquarius, the sign of universal consciousness.

Initiation: the process of penetrating into the mysteries of the science of the Self and of one's self in all senses. The Path of Initiation is the final stage in the evolution traveled by man, and is divided into seven stages represented by the seven gateways of the chakras.

Intelligences,
listening: the devas who pick up that particular note, and tone from the transmitters of the physical plane sound, which is needed to gather the substance for any intended material form.

Intuition: the ability to arrive at knowledge through the link established between the personality and the soul. It is achieved through the extension of the reasoning faculty; it is the sense of synthesis; the ability to think in wholes and to touch the world of causes.

Involution: the path taken by spirit through the four worlds to be solidly immersed into matter in the world of Assiah.

Isis: one of the three aspects of the Virgin Mother; She symbolizes the aspect of the form of Nature called the personality vehicle, and specifically the manifestation of the Christ Child, on the emotional or astral plane.

Israel: the peoples of the Earth who are descendants of the three older brothers of the Race; they are: Arabs, Semites, Afghans, Moors; the Latin and Celtic peoples; the Teutons, Scandinavians and Anglo-Saxons.

Jehovah: He who is God; the Masculine aspect of Jehovah Elohim.

Jerusalem: that place symbolically in the individual, country, and the world where death to separation and ignorance takes place; the Abode of Peace; that place arrived at by the regenerated consciousness; the sign of Pisces is symbolically Jerusalem.

Jews: being of the tribe of Judah bearing certain spiritual characteristics, and having divine responsibilities; they are a remnant of the all the peoples and races of the world.

Karma: the Law of Action and Reaction; Saturn, known as the Lord of Karma.

Knower, the: the Initiate; one who has achieved self-knowledge.

Kundalini: the coiled-up serpent energy at the base of the spine, which eventually unfurls during the process of spiritual awakening. This force opens the spiritual centers along the spine, releasing spiritual fire, which activates the centers in the head for receiving the higher knowledge into the body.

Law of Attraction: it is the primary Law of man, and governs the material process of form building; it describes the compelling force of attraction that holds our solar system to the Sirian System; holds our planets revolving around our central unit, the Sun; its other half is the Law of Repulsion.

Liberation,
Path of: achieved through the evolutionary unfoldment or gradual development, which leads to the final stages through the Rod of Initiation.

Libido: the Scorpio energy in the body; when lifted up and transformed to the level of the soul, awakens the aspirant to beneficent expressions

Logarithmic spiral: a form, which retains the essence of pastimes, while the form expands.

Lodge, the: as a room, it is an oblong square and represents one-half of a perfect square and the lower half of a circle. These are symbolic of the unregenerated man who is not yet "whole". Similarly, the planet Earth and the human body are considered a "Lodge" and are moving toward wholeness. When the candidate becomes a Master Mason, he has "squared the circle", and has become the perfect stone and the "chief corner stone", a cube. He is now the "Keystone".

Lodge, the Blue: the Sirian Lodge is the true Blue Lodge, in which the candidate in this lodge has to become a lowly aspirant with all the true and full initiations awaiting him, within the sunshine of the major Sun.

Lodge, Great White: its organized efforts are directed toward lifting the organized forces of materialism to a higher and spiritual plane.

Lodge of Messengers: a custodian of the truth as it is in Christ; those whose task it is to save the world, to impart revelation, and to demonstrate divinity.

Logos: the Deity who manifests through every nation and people. Metaphysically, speech is the logos of thought and is translated as the "word."

Lucifer: the Sun of the morning and the head of the Center of Humanity; the prince of the power of the Air; the twin aspect of Archangel Michael.

Lunar: pertaining to the Moon; the High Priestess is a lunar symbol, and relates to the pituitary gland; under the direction of the Lunar Lords, the Builders work to create form.

Malkuth: the tenth sphere on the Tree of Life; the root of the Tree is in Kether, and the fruits of the Tree are in Malkuth.

Many-ness: the manifold outward expression of the Oneness, the Divine Idea in the world of matter.

Mary: the third of the three goddesses related to the mother aspect, who brought the Christ child down to the plane of incarnation, the physical plane; the Mother of "the Corner Stone."

Master Mason: the man or woman who has taken the final initiation and has become an adept of whom Hiram Abiff is a type. S/he is the Knower and Master Builder of the Lodge.

Melchizedek: the Ancient of Days or the Great High Priest.

Mercury: the Roman name for Thoth or Hermes. The name of the metal associated with the pineal gland.

Messiah: the Redeemer; Gematria suggests that the numeration of the serpent who tempted

Eve, is identical with the numeration of the Messiach, the Messiah.

Metatron: the Great and Mighty Tree of Life; Metaroneth or Shekinah— the way to the Tree who is Divine Grace; interchangeably with God and the Archangel; Jehovah— "the Master" and the Ambassador.

Money: the concretized expression of the third type of spiritual energy.

Mongolians: the primary members of the Fourth Root Race or Fourth Life Wave; includes the Turks.

Moon Center, the: associated with the sixth chakra, and the pituitary gland. This center oversees the development of all forms.

Moses: in its esoteric Egyptian sense— one who has been admitted into the Mystery Schools of Wisdom and has gone forth to teach the ignorant, concerning the gods and the mysteries of life as taught in the temples of Osiris, Isis, and Serapis.

Mother, the Dark: related to the Black Pillar in Solomon's Temple; the sphere of Saturn; Binah, who is known as the limiting, restricting influence in life; the reflective or shadow aspect.

Mount Sinai: the Mountain of the Moon, said to be the monument of the exact time of the lunar years and months by which this spiritual vitalizing cycle could be computed; is related to Hagar, the bond woman and mother of Ishmael.

Mutable Cross, the: sometimes called "the Cross of Rebirth", which emphasis the constant mutations of which it is the symbol; it is also the " Cross of Changing Lives".

Mystery of Faith: the union of Male and Female in the Ineffable persons, causing conception and birth everlasting; the union of Jehovah and Elohim, which is the source of all other Mysteries.

Mystery of Sex: the Mystery of Shekinah; Supreme Wisdom.

Neptune: as agent of the Heart of the Sun, which pours its energies through this planet upon man, and produces the development of mystical consciousness, or that innate sensitivity that leads to the higher vision; known esoterically as the initiator; a synthesizing planet.

Occult: that which is hidden or veiled; secret knowledge.

Octahedron: one of the five Platonic or Pythagorean solids, with eight equilateral triangles as faces.

Oneness: the state of union with the negative and positive poles.

Osiris: though not the Sun, is the vital principle of Nature, which the ancients associate with this Egyptian Deity; his symbol, the opened eye, is used in honor of the Sun, the Great Eye of the universe.

P.A.L., Brother: the Brother with whom Brother C.R.C. became acquainted on his way to the Holy Land; a distinctive quality of Brother P.A.L.

is his determination to achieve initiation, which is to get to the Holy Land.

Path of Liberation: the journey that leads the soul out of darkness into light or out of ignorance into knowledge; in his struggle for mastery, he is willing to sacrifice even unto death.

Path of Return: the conscious path of humanity in the journey back into full consciousness along the thirty-two paths of wisdom.

Pentagram: the five-pointed geometric symbol of spirit and its dominion over matter: Ether, Fire, Water, Air and Earth.

Personality vehicle: the combined physical, emotional and mental bodies.

Philosophers, Fire: a term associated with the true Rosicrucians.

Philosopher's Stone: the stone that the builder refused; is associated with Mary, the Mother of the Corner Stone; the Elixir of Immortality.

Phoenix, the: a symbol of immortality of the soul and alchemical transmutation; usually referred to in the Mysteries with the initiate or men who are born again; just as physical birth gives man consciousness in the physical world, the candidate, after nine degrees in the womb of the Mysteries, is born to consciousness into a consciousness of the spiritual world.

Physical Sun, the: is associated with multiplicity, and the animal soul; one of the three aspects of the sun, which is a factor that brings consciousness to the birth and makes the ultimate goal attainable; makes all forms of consciousness possible.

Pleiades: the constellation representing the third aspect of the Godhead. It is associated with Binah on the Tree of Life; called the seven sisters or the seven rays of life energy manifesting on our planet.

Planets: the 12 known bodies of energy forces in the solar system that impact the growth and evolution of all life on Earth; there are seven sacred and five non-sacred planets, which include Vulcan and Earth.

Platonic solids: also called Pythagorean solids, which are five in number proceeding from the sphere of Akasha; they are: the Tetrahedron, the Octahedron, the Cube, the Icosahedron, and the Dodecahedron.

Polaris: the polestar or North Star; Alpha in the constellation of Ursa Minor.

Pole Star, the: The North Star: Polaris

Polyhedras: solids bounded by plane faces.

Poverty: defined in occultism as being in a state of delusion; opposed to one's true self, separated from God and his fellowman, and is driven by one's five-senses, three- dimensional consciousness.

Prana: The Life Principle; the Life Breath; active radiatory heat which varies in vibration and quality according to the receiving Entity.

Prima Materia: alchemical water; the primal substance from which all life emerged.

Primordial: an elementary principle; first in the order of development or growth of an organism.

Principles,
Seven Hermetic: the seven divine laws on which manifestation is established— Mentalism, Correspondence, Vibration, Polarity, Rhythm, Cause and Effect, and Gender.

Principle,
the Feminine : the negative aspect of the Divine pair; Elohim; Isis.

Principle,
the Masculine: the positive aspect of the divine pair; Jehovah; Osiris.

Prithivi: one of the five Twattas representing the element of Earth.

Prodigal Son: a symbol for humanity; the wandering Jew who left his father's house to achieve an expansion of consciousness through experiment and experience.

Proportion, Extreme
and Mean: the division of a quantity that will make its lesser part to its greater part, as the greater part is to the whole; the proportion 5:8 is the nearest arithmetic expression of this; also called the Extreme Mean Ratio.

Pyramid,
the Great: a stone emblem of the Eternal Flame, the Egyptians call "the Light".

Pythagorean
triangle: consists of a vertical line assigned to the Alchemical Father or Osiris of three units;

a base of four units assigned to Isis, the Alchemical Mother; and a hypotenuse of five units assigned to Horus, the Alchemical Child.

Qabalah: the traditional Hermetic and Judaic sciences called the mathematics of human thought; the algebra of faith that solves all problems of the soul as equations, by isolating the unknowns; it brings to ideas the clarity and rigorous exactitude of numbers and its results for the mind are infallibility, relative to the sphere of human knowledge; for the heart it provides profound peace; it is said to have its origin in Egypt.

Quintessence: Spirit, the essence of all there is.

Raphael, archangel: the archangel who rules the eastern quadrant of the heavens. "God, the Healer-of-Mind."

Rays: the seven streams of force or great lights of the Logos. Each Ray is the embodiment of a great cosmic entity.

R. C.: meaning, *roke*: the development of the character, mark or seal of compassion, and tenderness, a result of Brother R.C.'s occult training.

River Jordan: Qabalistic alchemists associate this river with the "Water of Minerals"; is also associated with the bloodstream of man.

Root Race, fourth: one of the seven races of man, which evolved upon the planet during a specific great cycle of planetary existence; the Chinese, Japanese, the Mongolians, and the Turks.

Root Race, fifth: the Aryan Race which is the Fifth Life Wave represented by the seven churches of Asia Minor: the Arch-Indian branch; the Arch-Persians; the Chaldean-Egyptian-Semetic; the Grecian-Latin-Roman; the Teuton-Anglo-Saxon; the Slavic; and the Manichean.

Root Race, third: emerged when individualization took place through polar relationships, and the scientific laws were understood; inhabitants of Lemuria, which extended from Madagascar, Ceylon and Sumatra, and included portions of now Africa, Fiji, Solomon Islands, New Guinea and stretched from the Indian Ocean to Australia.

Rosicrucian,
Invisible Order: it is invisible because it has no external organization; its members are men and women on earth in physical bodies; they are invisible to ordinary eyes, because the minds behind those eyes cannot recognize the marks of a true Rosicrucian.

Rosicrucian Grade: a mark of attainment in the training and development of the candidate in the occult mysteries toward Initiation.

Sabbath: pertaining to Saturn; the seventh day of the week; the seventh year; period of rest.

Sacred Geometry: diagrams based on the division of the circle into four quarters, and all the parts and elements involved are interrelated into a unified design, which are usually cosmological, and represent the essential structure of the universe.

Sage: a seer; an adept; an Initiate; a Master of Compassion and Wisdom.

Salt: alchemists declare that this was the first created substance, produced by fire out of God; in salt, all of creation is concentrated, and in salt, is the establishment of the beginning and end of all things; the cube is the form associated with this substance; it is one of the three principles of creation. Together with Mercury, and Sulphur they constitute the three Principles of the Alchemical Father and each is said to exist in each other.

Saturn: associated with Saturday; Binah; is referred to as the Lord of Karma, the imposer of retribution; takes the candidate to the mountain of initiation in the sign of Capricorn.

Self-consciousness: the awareness in the individual of purpose, of a self-directed life, and of a developed and definite life-plan and program. These are indicative of some measure of integration and mental perception.

Septenate: sevenfold; man and all forms are controlled by septenate energies, which are a rule in the inner government of our universe and our solar system.

Seven Churches of
Asia Minor: related to the seven branches of the Aryan Race, the Fifth Life Wave; they are: Ephesus: the Arch-Indian branch; Smyrna: the Arch-Persians; Pergamos: the Chaldean-

Egyptian-Semetic; Thyatira: the Grecian-Latin-Roman; Sardia: the Teuton-Anglo-Saxon; Philadelphia: the Slavic; and Laodicea: the Manichean.

Shamballa: the city of the Gods and home of the mystical occult doctrine; the custodian of the plan for our planet.

Sheath, causal: the fires manifest through these veils of substance, which hide and conceal the inner Reality.

Shekinah: the mystery of God and Man; of Man in the likeness of the Elohim, and of the relation between things above and things below; the intercourse of union upon earth performed in the spirit of celestial union.

Sixteen: the age at which the physical transformations of puberty were completed to allow for a safe beginning of the undertaking that prepares Brother C.R.C. for occult initiation.

SPR: sepher; Book M; the *Liber Mundi*; the Book; Gematria gives Brother C.R.C. and *The Book* the same value, implying that the regenerated body of Brother C.R.C. is one and the same with the Book of Life.

Sirius: called the "dog star". Vibrations from Sirius reach our planet via the cosmic mental plane. It is the Star of Sensitivity governing the Hierarchy.

Solomon's Seal: the interlaced Star of David or hexagram.

Solomon's Temple: a symbolic form of the deathless physical body not made with hands and built out of the ruins of the previously destroyed temples, the personality and the soul; finally the Master Mason, or Hiram Abiff, stands as that perfected Temple.

Soul, the: the Higher Self or Higher Mind. It projects out into form through the personality vehicle to be used for carrying out of the divine plan in matter. It is the medium between Spirit and Matter; ultimately, it too must die.

Sphere, the: the most perfect of all created forms.

Sphinx: a combination of woman and lion; signify the composite nature of man; a symbol of the attainment of the adept, who has solved the riddle of life.

Spirits, seven: Anael; Raphael; Gabriel; Tsaphkiel; Tzadkiel; Kamael; and Michael.

Sun, Central Spititual: a symbol of Unity; the awareness of God; the will of the whole.

Swastika: the mutable cross of material change and constant movement. The swastika can be a symbol for evil, and the false use of matter.

Teja: one of the five Twattas, representing the element of fire.

Tetrahedron: one of the five Platonic or Pythagorean solids, with four equilateral triangles as faces.

Thinker, the: the Heavenly Man who is also a Knower; the adept, he imposes rhythm upon every human atom.

Third Order, the: Wise Men who are actual human beings and who constitute the Invisible Rosicrucian

Fraternity; *and* designated as Masters, because they actually do exercise mastery over all things and creatures that are naturally subordinate to man.

Thirteenth Path: the path, and the only one that leads to the grade of Ipsissimus, which means "he who is most himself"; is associated with Gimel, meaning "Camel", and is assigned to the High Priestess, the Intelligence of Unity, and Love. This path leads to the complete re-collection of what he is, and the perpetual remembrance that "the Lord is in his Holy Temple."

Tree of Knowledge of Good and of Evil: represents imbalance or polarity, and the secret of mortality

Tree of Life: the glyph of man and the universe. This geometric symbol consists of ten Sephiroth or emanations and twenty-two secret paths, constituting the thirty-two paths of wisdom.

Triangle, equilateral: symbol of Spirit, of Deity, and its Triune Nature; the three in One; connection with the sacred delta, composed of three equal lines, and three equal angles.

Twenty-seven: the magical age at which Brother C.R. becomes the Basis or Foundation of the Fraternity; the alchemical age when the idea for the reformation of the arts and sciences became clear in his mind.

Turks: primary members of the Fourth Root Race; they helped to awaken the physical and mental powers in Brother C. R. C. that were submerged; characteristic of the Fourth Life Wave.

Unicorn: spiritually it symbolizes the "fighting and triumphant creature" of the ancient myths in which the lion, the king of beasts, is blinded and killed by the piercing of his eye and heart, by the long horn of the unicorn; the dual horns of the Goat become the single horn of the Unicorn on the mountaintop of initiation; associated with the pineal gland.

Uniting Intelligence: the thirteenth path of the High Priestess and of memory; the path that leads from Tiphareth to Kether on the Tree of Life; the path of the perfect memory of the One Identity, which is the link that unites all personalities.

Uranus: the ruler of the Age of Aquarius; the producer of occult consciousness, which is the intelligent fusing condition; produces the scientific at-one-ment of the higher and lower selves, through the intelligent use of the mind.

Vayu: one of the five Twattas and represents the element of air.

Vesica Piscis: the space created by the intersection of two circles of equal radius, within which an equilateral triangle can be constructed; the basis of some of the most important geometric secrets of operative masons; the proportions of the Vesica Piscis and the equilateral triangle were used in the construction of many cathedrals and in architecture of the Middle Ages.

Venus: the alter ego of the planet Earth; the mental energy of humanity that establishes the relation of man-to-man and nation-to-nation. Venus is to Earth, what the Higher Self is to the Personality.

Virgo: this constellation is the symbol of the woman clothed with the sun, with the moon under her feet, and upon her head, a crown of twelve stars; represents Isis; the sign under which the whole goal of the evolutionary process, which is to shield, nurture, and finally reveal the hidden spiritual reality, is made manifest.

Wisdom,
Master of: one who has reached the sublime degree of Master Mason, the wages of those who travel East on the Camel (*Gimel*) of earnest desire.

World-Wide-Web: the connecting link, and the Great Spider Web, created by the Divine Mother to connect man-to-man, and nation-to-nation; this creation of the builders is meant to merge the realms of light with those of darkness.

Yeshua: Jesus the Christ that means, "Self-existence liberates"; the inherent tendency toward liberty, which is at the heart of the cosmic order.

Zohar: a collection that is termed by Qabalists "the Work of the Chariot", "the Work of Creation"; the Sepher Yetzirah, which is supposed to embody a Tradition handed down from the time of Abraham.

Index

237

D

N

O

P

Pain, 28
Paracelsus, 79, 123
Path of Discipleship, 106
Path of Illumination, 84
Path of Initiation, 124
Path of Return, 68, 69, 70,
 86, 114
Peh, 187
Pentagon, the, 32
Pentecost, xxi
Perfect Mediatrix, 151
Permanent Atoms, 67
Perpetual Intelligence, 45,
 152
Pharaoh, 142
Philosopher's Stone, 83,
 190
Philosophers, 40, 77
Philosophical Work, 80, 83
Phoenix, the, 84
Physical Man, the, 85
Physical Sun, the, 108
Pillar of cloud by day, 135
Pillar of fire by night, 135
Pillar of Wisdom, 166
Pineal body, 93, 167
Piscean Cycle, 69
Piscean World Saviors, 74
Pisces, 68
Pituitary body, 129, 167
Pituitary gland, 93
Planetary Etheric Web, 63
Planetary Lords of the Solar
 System, the
Platonic Solids, 43, 45, 54
Pleiades, the, 89, 127
Pluto, 69

Pointer in the Great Bear,
 125
Pointers, the, 106
Polaris, 125
Pole Star, 106, 125
Polyhedras, the five, 43
Poverty, 162
Practical Occultism, 130
Prakriti, 175
Prana, 95
Prana, undifferentiated, 129
Pranic Emanations, 60
Prima Materia, 79
Primal Fire, 30
Primal Will, 165
Primordial form, 42
Primordial Intelligent Life,
 30
Primordial substance, 81
Principle of Cause and
 Effect, 92
Principle of
 Correspondence,
 91
Principle of Gender, 93
Principle of Mentalism, 91
Principle of Polarity, 91
Principle of Rhythm, 92
Principle of Vibration, 91
Prithivi, 47
Prodigal Son, 70, 108, 112,
 164
Promised Land, 135
Prophet Daniel, 188
Proportionality, 49
Pulmonary artery, 117
Pulmonary veins, 117
Pythagoras, 40, 163
Pythagorean, right triangle,
 43, 44

Q

Qoph, 184
Queen, xxii
Quicksilver, 93
Quintessence, 43, 45, 47

R

Radiatory emanations, 71
Rama Prasad, 45
Raphael, 93
Rectangle, 41
Rectangular square, 41
Redemption, xxiii
Regenerated Man, 45, 65,
    179
Regina Angelorum, 141
Repositories of past
    experiences, 67
Resch, 111
River Jordan, the, 84, 171
River of Souls, 149
Robert Lawlor, 44
Roke, 178
Root of Matter, 74
Rosicrucian Order of
    Initiates, 160
Rule of Brotherhood, 104

S

Sabbath, 138
Sacred Geometry, 42
Sagittarius, 68
Sais, 190
Salamanders, 61
Salt Crystal, 41
Salt, 45, 80

Salvation, 37
Sarcophagus, 50
Satan, 102
Saturday, 94
Saturn, 54, 66, 94, 101,
    103, 161
Scapegoat, 29
Scepter of power, 124, 125
Scorpio region of the body,
    83
Scorpio, 107
Scroll, xxii, 101
Seat of Life, 122
Second Birth, 81
Secret place at the center,
    96
Seeing elementals, 62
Self-consciousness, 158
Self-knowledge, 39, 47
Sense of hearing, 46
Sense of sight, 46
Sense of smell, 46
Sense of taste, 46
Sense of touch, 46
Sensitivity, 123
Separation, 28
Sepirothic Tree, 138
Septenate, 30
Serpent power, 161
Seven Churches of Asia
    Minor, 166
Seven Cosmic Centers, 61
Seven Councils, 90
Seven Governors, 90
Seven Hermetic Principles,
    91
Seven Rishis, 89
Seven Seals, 101
Seven Sisters, 89
Seven Spirits Before the
    Throne, 120

About the Author

⟡〰️⟡

Unveiling the Secrets of the Feminine Principle was written to reveal the Great Mysteries of the Shekinah, the Divine Mother. She is the Third Aspect of the Divine Triad — the Holy Ghost, the Comforter. She is who the Scriptures predicted would come at the dawning of the Aquarian Age to establish the Kingdom of Heaven on Earth and restore the balance of power and equality between the Masculine and the Feminine. She is here to initiate the Age of Peace, which can only be achieved through private and public systems based on justice and brotherhood. To achieve this, the female aspect of life must not only have a voice but also an equal place in the decisions and policies which impact all aspects of human life and without which, the Divine Plan for the liberation of humanity cannot be achieved.

Etta is the author of *'Understanding Your Choice'*, a compilation of the Arcane Mysteries which she completed in 2001. Her third book, *'The Role of Consciousness in Governance'* to be completed by early 2008, will explain how the Divine Will and Plan for humanity must be manifested on Earth through the governments of all countries, in order for the divine destiny of humanity to become a reality.

She is the founder of the 'Institute for Conscious Global Change', a non-profit organization dedicated to making the needs of all peoples in all countries more visible. This will be accomplished through the Virtual Global Project, which creates virtually the world we envision with accurate, concrete, on-going data being provided to keep the world informed and to recommend change in each locale. This virtual image of a new world and its peoples will help to precipitate those mental images into the physical world.

Etta holds a B.A. degree in Biology, a M.S. degree in Psychoanalytic Counseling and Development and another in Administrative Leadership and Supervision.

She has one daughter and one grandson.

Made in the USA
Las Vegas, NV
11 June 2021